Praise for *Vigil: Hong Kong on the Brink*

"A remarkable, and remarkably succinct, analysis of the ongoing crisis in Hong Kong. This is essential reading for understanding China's foreign policy, the legacies of empire, and above all the extraordinary politics, society, and culture of contemporary Hong Kong."

—**Julia Lovell,**
Professor of modern China
at Birkbeck, University of London
and author of *Maoism: A Global History*

"Jeffrey Wasserstrom has long been a master of unearthing shared resonances in the human experience across ages and in different societies. With *Vigil*, he has not only produced a surefooted guide to the turmoil shaking Hong Kong, but a richly insightful look at how recent events there fit into the broader sweep of history."

—**Howard W. French,**
author of *Everything Under
the Heavens: How the Past Helps
Shape China's Push for Global Power*

"This is an essential primer to understand the factors driving the most serious challenge to Beijing since the 1989 protest movement. Written clearly and concisely, it offers a handy background briefing to Hong Kong's political crisis."

—**Louisa Lim,**
author of *The People's Republic
of Amnesia and Tiananmen Revisited*

"A concise yet pertinent analysis of why and how Hong Kong exploded into months of escalating protests in 2019. Wasserstrom combines the deep knowledge of a historian and the captivating voice of literary writing. The result is an account that weaves together objective historical parallels and subjective sentiments that have driven Hong Kong's various waves of protest."

—Victoria Tin-bor Hui,
Associate Professor, Department of
Political Science, University of Notre Dame

Vigil
Hong Kong
on the Brink

COLUMBIA GLOBAL REPORTS
NEW YORK

Vigil
Hong Kong
on the Brink

Jeffrey Wasserstrom

With Contributions by Amy Hawkins

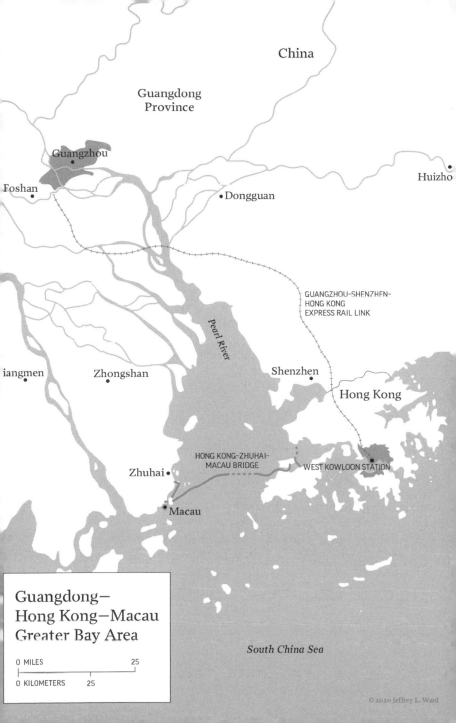

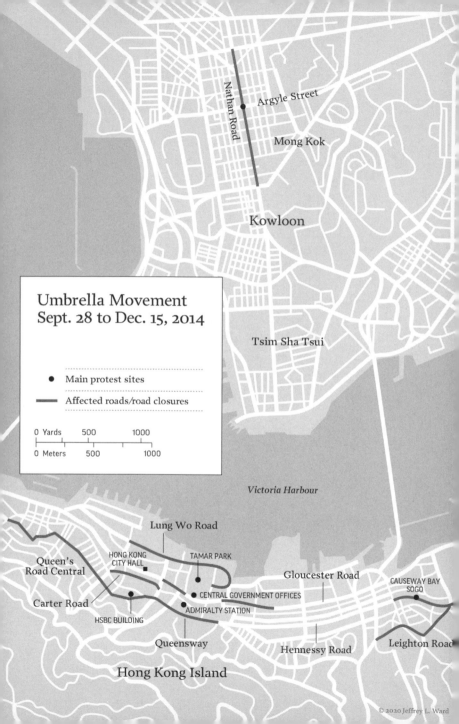

Umbrella Movement
Sept. 28 to Dec. 15, 2014

● Main protest sites

━━ Affected roads/road closures

0 Yards   500   1000
0 Meters   500   1000

Nathan Road

● Argyle Street

Mong Kok

Kowloon

Tsim Sha Tsui

Victoria Harbour

Lung Wo Road

Queen's
Road Central

HONG KONG
CITY HALL

TAMAR PARK

Gloucester Road

CAUSEWAY BAY
SOGO

Carter Road

● CENTRAL GOVERNMENT OFFICES

HSBC BUILDING

ADMIRALTY STATION

Queensway

Hennessy Road

Leighton Road

Hong Kong Island

© 2020 Jeffrey L. Ward

China

Guangdong
Province

Hong Kong

Yuen Long

Tuen Mun

New Territories

Sha Tin

Airport

Kowloon

Lantau Island

Hong Kong Island

2019 Major Protests

○ July
◯ August
◉ September
● October

South China Sea

0 Miles   5
0 Kilometers   10

© 2020 Jeffrey L. Ward

Published with support from the Stavros Niarchos Foundation (SNF)

ΙΣΝ/SNF ΙΔΡΥΜΑ ΣΤΑΥΡΟΣ ΝΙΑΡΧΟΣ
STAVROS NIARCHOS FOUNDATION

Vigil
Hong Kong on the Brink

Published by Columbia Global Reports
91 Claremont Avenue, Suite 515
New York, NY 10027
globalreports.columbia.edu
facebook.com/columbiaglobalreports
@columbiaGR

Library of Congress Control Number: 2019953002
ISBN: 978-1-7336237-4-2
E-book ISBN: 978-1-7336237-5-9

Book design by Strick&Williams
Map design by Jeffrey L. Ward
Author photograph by Steve Zylius

Printed in the United States of America

CONTENTS

Disappearances

Hong Kong and West Berlin stand at opposite ends of the Eurasian landmass, about as far apart as two cities can be geographically and culturally. And yet for most of the second half of the twentieth century, they were doppelgangers in an important way. Each was a focal point of Cold War tensions, linked by the shared stresses and strains of being battlegrounds between two diametrically opposed ideologies. Hong Kong, like West Berlin, was used as a listening post onto a nearby place. This parallel was not lost on John le Carré. When the author of *The Spy Who Came in from the Cold* decided to set a novel in Asia in the late 1970s, he opened *The Honourable Schoolboy* with Hong Kong scenes involving information gatherers—some spies, some journalists—who were intently interested in the People's Republic of China.

During the final dozen years of the last century, the unwinding of the Cold War changed each city in a profound way. For Berlin, Germany's reunification in 1990 made the city whole again. It is now Germany's capital and the country's most important metropolis. Walking or driving around Berlin in 2019, you can move between what were once parts of two very different cities without necessarily noticing you have done so, as long as no landmarks associated with the Berlin Wall are in sight. Checkpoint Charlie is now a museum, and the last guard tower near the Wall on the other side, from which East German soldiers sometimes shot at escapees heading for the West, is the focus of a historical preservation effort. When it comes to magazines and newspapers, it makes no difference in twenty-first-century Berlin where exactly you are in the city when you want to buy one. If you prefer digitally digestible forms of information, the web works identically east and west of the old Wall.

The Hong Kong story is different. In 1997, Britain handed over its prized colony to the People's Republic of China, making it a Special Administrative Region that was supposed to enjoy a "high degree of autonomy" for fifty years. Freedoms of speech, assembly, and protest are still protected in Hong Kong under the territory's constitution, called the Basic Law. This was to be a grand experiment—these freedoms are not available anywhere on the Chinese mainland! In Hong Kong, you can buy biographies of and writings by the Dalai Lama. Hong Kong newspapers run articles that criticize and cartoons that mock top leaders of China's Communist Party. The Great Firewall makes surfing the web a very different experience on opposite sides of the border. If you are in the mainland, unless you use a VPN to help you scale the digital wall, you get no access to Twitter, Facebook, the *New York Times,* or specialized sites devoted to such varied things as *The Gate of Heavenly Peace,* a documentary about the Tiananmen protests and June 4 Massacre of 1989, and the *Shen*

14   *Yun* pageant that is linked to the banned Falun Gong sect. By
contrast, those who come to Hong Kong from Toronto, Toledo,
Lisbon, or London are likely to notice little difference between
using the web at home and doing so there—except that their
internet connection will likely be faster than they are used to
and their internet provider's reach more extensive.

But in subtle and not so subtle ways, some old differences
between how lives used to be lived on opposite sides of the
border separating Hong Kong from the mainland began to blur
or disappear late in the last century. A new high-speed train
that connects Hong Kong to Shenzhen and Guangzhou, called
the Express Rail Link, illustrates this. The Handover deal that
Whitehall and Beijing struck in 1984 stipulated that Hong
Kong would be able to maintain a separate legal system, under
a framework known as "One Country, Two Systems," until
2047. According to the Basic Law, "No department of the Central People's Government and no province, autonomous region,
or municipality directly under the Central Government may
interfere in the affairs which the Hong Kong Special Administrative Region administers on its own." But in part of a new
Express Rail Link terminal in Hong Kong that opened in 2018,
called the West Kowloon Station, all security is handled by
mainland employees, and, for the first time on Hong Kong soil,
travelers are subject to mainland Chinese laws instead of Hong
Kong laws.

And if you buy a SIM card for your cell phone and you want
it to work in Hong Kong as well as in Macau (the former Portuguese colony that in 1999 followed its neighbor in becoming
a Special Administrative Region of China), as I did during my
most recent visit to the cities, you may find on the packaging

the words "Big Bay Area 10-Day Pre-paid Sim Card" in large
type. What this promises users is that they will be able to use
the card not just in Hong Kong and Macau (where in recent years
there has been more political and press freedom than in mainland cities but less than in Hong Kong), but also in cities across
the border, like Zhuhai, Guangzhou, and Shenzhen, which are
also located in the Pearl River Delta, recently termed the Greater
Bay Area. The Greater Bay Area plan to integrate Hong Kong and
Macau with mainland cities is scheduled to move toward com-
pletion in the 2020s, and includes large-scale development and
infrastructure plans that were already in place even before the
plan was announced in 2019: The Express Rail Link is a case in
point, and the Hong Kong–Zhuhai–Macau Bridge, an enormous thirty-four-mile-long bridge and tunnel system that
is the longest sea crossing in the world, also opened in 2018.
The project's vision is of a time when going from one Special
Administrative Region to the other and either of them to mainland cities will be as effortless and seem as natural as going from
San Francisco to Oakland to Silicon Valley in the Bay Area on
the other side of the Pacific.

"We will no longer be Hong Kong people, but Greater Bay
Area people," Jonathan Choi Koon-shum, chairman of the
local Chinese General Chamber of Commerce, told a journalist in a 2018 interview. He saw this as having the potential
to be a very positive development, and he encouraged local residents to "focus on integration rather than on the interests of
Hong Kong." Integration is, for some, such as Choi, the stuff that
dreams are made of, while it is a source of nightmares for others.

While using a Greater Bay Area SIM card to make phone
calls in various cities can be a seamless experience, this is not so

16   if I were to surf the web in Shenzhen—where I would have been
      unable to check out the *New York Times* or look for a Liu Xiaobo
      quote on a web page devoted to the film *The Gate of Heavenly
      Peace*, easy things to do in Hong Kong and Macau.

      I am left wondering if Hong Kong–based Greater Bay Area
      boosters, such as Choi, look forward to a time when the dig-
      ital border marked by the Great Firewall vanishes. And if they
      do, do they somehow imagine that surfing the web in Shenzhen
      will become just like surfing the web now is in Hong Kong and
      Macau? It is much more likely that the opposite would happen,
      and that both SARs would end up within the Great Firewall. Of
      course, while some find good reasons to fear and others find
      good reasons to look forward to disappearing borders of varying
      kinds, it is important to remember that there are still others
      who do not see the process as all that important. Consider, for
      example, the following exchange *Guardian* reporter Lily Kuo had
      in 2018 when writing a story about the way that new transpor-
      tation routes were making it less obvious when one moves from
      one part of the Pearl River Delta to another. "Lai Youyou, on her
      way to Hong Kong from Shenzhen with her friend to go shop-
      ping, shrugs when asked if she worries the distinction between
      Hong Kong and mainland China is disappearing. 'It's all the
      same,' she says. 'We can go there. They can come here.'"

      But it is not the same. The epic David-and-Goliath struggle cur-
      rently underway in Hong Kong which is the focus of this book,
      can be seen in part as rooted in contrasting views of the meaning
      and significance of borders and what happens as they blur or
      disappear. There are those who welcome the fading of distinc-
      tions between Hong Kong and mainland cities—or at least do

not worry about them much. This can be because they view the
Party as a benevolent organization, or for pragmatic reasons, as
is the case with some people who work in Hong Kong but live
in Shenzhen, where rents are not as astronomically high. On
the other side in the struggle are those who treasure the many
aspects of local life, including a more vibrant civil society and
courts that operate with more independence from other government bodies, that make Hong Kong distinctive—and freer.
For them, the mainland having direct and total control over part
of a train station located in the heart of Hong Kong conjures a
sense of outrage not so different from what a resident of West
Berlin might have felt on learning that Checkpoint Charlie was
to be controlled by the Stasi.

In 2015, five people associated with a publishing house and
bookstore known for producing gossipy, lightly sourced exposés
of the private lives of Beijing leaders went missing. One of them
was living in Thailand and held a Swedish passport when he
was taken onto the mainland, while others were living in Hong
Kong and did not have deep ties to any other place. They were
all involved with the sort of publications that were disliked
intensely by Xi Jinping and other Beijing leaders. Some of the
men were pressured into making televised "confessions" as the
price of regaining their freedom; one of the men, the holder of
Swedish citizenship, remains detained on the mainland, where
the authorities have rebuffed diplomatic entreaties on his
behalf, insisting that his Chinese origins renders his Swedish
citizenship irrelevant. This set of disappearances made head-
lines around the world, then was soon forgotten by many people
in other places as new crises occurred. But it is something that
continues to haunt many in Hong Kong.

The episode seems like a plot that a Le Carré wannabe might conjure up. The protest leader Agnes Chow, who was just nineteen, modified a famous verse by Martin Niemöller—about people failing to do enough when people begin to disappear, due to thinking that they are safe from sharing the same fate later on—in an early 2016 video that was watched within days by hundreds of thousands of people on YouTube. In Chow's reworking, it opens with the line "First they came for the activist," and goes on to refer to journalists and then booksellers being whisked away. Many activists that my colleague Amy Hawkins and I talked to are worried that Beijing and its local proxies will be able to arrest them openly in the future, without having to resort to Carré-esque cloak-and-dagger subterfuge.

It is no longer just activists who are concerned about the issue of people disappearing across the border. This is shown by the size of the crowds made up of people from all walks of life that flooded the streets of Hong Kong throughout the late spring and summer of 2019 and continue to do so into the fall. Varied grievances are inspiring people to turn out for events, and what has convinced some Hong Kongers to take part in many gatherings is anger that the police were too aggressive in handling previous ones. Still, the original trigger for the recent series of marches—gatherings that have solidified Hong Kong's reputation as a "city of protest," to borrow the title of a valuable 2017 book by local lawyer Antony Dapiran—is a proposed extradition law. Opponents of the bill have insisted that, if it is implemented, it would become far too easy for all kinds of local residents, and even for international travelers passing through, to disappear from Hong Kong and reappear in mainland prisons, with as little chance of a fair trial as a West Berlin resident would have had if he or she ended up being tried on the other side of the Wall for an act that displeased the heads of the Communist Party in East Germany or those in Moscow on whom the East German leaders depended and to whom they were beholden.

References to disappearances figured in many of the interviews that Hawkins and I conducted, during which we talked to people ranging from longtime residents to Chris Patten, the last governor of colonial Hong Kong. We asked people to name a novel or film that captured something important about Hong Kong's situation. The writer Ma Jian brought up George Orwell's *Nineteen Eighty-Four*, saying he formerly associated it only with the mainland, from which he has long been banned because of his novels about taboo topics. Due to the disappearance of the sense of safety he used to feel in Hong Kong, where he made his home before moving to London, he had begun to think of the city as part of Big Brother's domain as well.

Didi Kirsten Tatlow was born and raised in Hong Kong, but she spent much of her career reporting from Beijing, in part because of a long-held conviction that events there would be crucial in determining Hong Kong's future. She chose the film *In the Mood for Love* by Hong Kong auteur Wong Kar-wai, because it evokes a sense of dreams that cannot be realized. She calls this a "nostalgia for the future," a longing for the impossible. She does not see direct parallels between events happening now in Hong Kong and the plot of *In the Mood for Love*, which was released in 2000. The feeling of something almost within grasp but then forever out of reach that pervades the film, though, reminds her of when it was still possible to feel that British colonial control could disappear without being replaced by a new

20   form of colonialism. Her nostalgia for a never-to-be-realized future free of all colonial forms is one, she stressed to me, that appeals not just to locals of Chinese descent. It also holds an allure for some members of families who had no ties to China before moving to Hong Kong but who also were not British, tracing their roots back to distant places ranging from India to, in the case of her own family, continental Europe.

    Wong Yeung-tat, a leader of a political organization called Civic Passion and publisher of its affiliated *Passion Times* newspaper, brought up a very different sort of film: the Hollywood blockbuster *Titanic*. Interviewed by Amy Hawkins in May, he said that Hong Kong made him think of a setting where "the ship is sinking" but many onboard are "just enjoying the party," even as the vessel disappears under the waves.

    Twenty-one-year-old Yale student Hana Meihan Davis, the youngest Hong Konger we asked about the topic, stressed the relevance of the *Hunger Games* series of books and films for those, like her, who were born after the Handover. The three finger salute of resistance from one of the movies was adopted by some protesters in Hong Kong and also Thailand in 2014, but this was not why she brought up the dystopian series focusing on Katniss Everdeen when I spoke to her after she had spent the summer of 2019 interning with the *Washington Post* and writing about her native city's upheavals. She noted the all-or-nothing feeling of desperation in the *Hunger Games* saga, and the fact that some of the boldest actions were being taken by teenagers and hence rough contemporaries of the fictional Katniss—and in many cases, like her, female. Feeling that a way of life they treasured was disappearing, the novels and films could be viewed as a source of hope for victory (young fighters triumphing over

impossible odds) or a way of giving your all for a lost cause. The
slogan "If we burn, you burn with us" that became a common
one in Hong Kong last summer, she reminded me, comes from
the *Hunger Games.*

Several others mentioned a different dystopian text in
our interviews: *Ten Years.* This 2015 film is one in which several sorts of disappearances are central motifs. It is made up
of five segments, each by a different local director in his thirties, which present Hong Kong as it could be in 2025 if current
trends continue. One episode focuses on a taxi driver who only
speaks Cantonese—which has long been, along with English,
the lingua franca of Hong Kong—but has a child being taught
only Mandarin, which is the official language of the mainland.
He finds himself limited to looking for fares in some districts
due to his linguistic orientation, and he has a GPS system in his
car that stops recognizing the addresses he gives in his native
tongue. A language closely tied to local identity is disappearing.
The most controversial segment of the movie focuses on a frus-
trated elderly female protester who burns herself alive. The
implication of this turn to self-immolation, a tactic that in the
PRC context is linked above all to Tibet—which was originally
promised considerable autonomy from Beijing but later became
one of the most tightly controlled parts of the PRC—is that
much more could disappear in the future. Given the role that
attacks on a locally valued language have played in repression
in Xinjiang as well as Tibet, by the time the credits to *Ten Years*
roll, some audience members may be thinking of both western
territories that are seen as places where Beijing has more often
used an iron-fist rather than velvet-glove approach to rule.
When the movie was up for a prize in Hong Kong, Beijing was

22   so determined to limit the spread of information about it that,
even though the awards program in question had been shown on
television on both sides of the border in the past, the planned
broadcast of it on the mainland disappeared from the schedule.

Spending time in Hong Kong in recent years, there are
people I have wanted to meet or see again who have disappeared
into jail cells. An interest in what has disappeared in Hong
Kong, what has not disappeared, and what could disappear in
the future provided a background for my most recent trip to the
territory in early June of 2019. I was determined to get to Hong
Kong ahead of the thirtieth anniversary of 1989's June Fourth
Massacre. As long as I was in Hong Kong by June 3, I would be
able to take part in a tradition that I feared someday might be
added to the ever-growing list of things that used to be part
of the Hong Kong political landscape but had subsequently
disappeared. This is a vigil held in Victoria Park in Causeway
Bay to commemorate the death of the many people—at least
hundreds, probably thousands—who soldiers of the People's
Liberation Army killed late at night on June 3 and early in the
morning of June 4, 1989. Despite devoting much of my career to
the study of Chinese student movements, including the Tiananmen struggle, I had never been in Hong Kong when this ceremony took place.

To worry about a future in which June Fourth vigils cannot
be held in Hong Kong, or can only be held in a less central and
less impressive setting than Victoria Park, which is located
in the heart of Hong Kong Island, is justified. Since 1989, no
public commemorations of the June Fourth Massacre have been
allowed anywhere on the mainland. And in recent years, far from
relaxing the policing of the anniversary date, the authorities

have even moved to curtail private mourning of the martyrs in cities such as Beijing.

I am glad I took part in this year's vigil. When the crowd fell silent midway through that gathering and I joined others in holding up a candle in memory of the martyrs, it was a magical moment. The glow of flickering flames on the ground combined with the twinkle of stars and glows from tall buildings nearby to create a unique spectacle in a city known for its glittering light displays. The mood throughout the event was solemn but with an undertone of hopefulness. The turnout of around 180,000 people was not quite as large as at the biggest previous vigil, but it was bigger than expected and surpassed the size of the crowd in the last couple of years. Attendees attributed this to growing outrage over the proposed extradition law that many people in Hong Kong felt was a direct assault on the "One Country, Two Systems" framework.

Most of the speeches delivered and songs sung at the vigil looked backward to tragic acts of violence that had happened in the past, but with the extradition law on the minds of attendees the event not surprisingly ended on a forward-looking note. Speakers called on the crowd to remember to take part in the march planned for the coming Sunday. Outrage over the extradition bill was palpable at the vigil and continued to grow in the days that followed, so it was no surprise that when the time came many attendees of the vigil heeded the call of the speakers, as did an enormous number of people who had not been at Victoria Park. The fight against the bill came to seem a life and death matter. This was reinforced by the fact that, in Cantonese, the main three-character term for "anti-extradition," while literally meaning "opposed sending to China," includes

24   two characters that are homophones for "send off a dying rel-
     ative" and also "give someone a clock" (slang for wishing death
     on the recipient). On June 9, two days after I left Hong Kong, an
     estimated one million people took to the streets to show how
     determined they were not to let their community die without a
     fight. A week after that, an even more massive march took place.
     Involving more than a quarter of the city's 7.4 million residents,
     it was not just the biggest protest gathering in Hong Kong's his-
     tory, but among the largest in the history of the world.

Negotiations

Perhaps the furthest back in time we can go to find a noteworthy underestimation and memorably mistaken prediction
about Hong Kong is to a letter dated April 21, 1841. "It is with
great regret that I express to you my extreme disappointment at
your Negotiations," Lord Palmerston, who was then serving the
second of his three terms as foreign secretary, would go on to
preside over Great Britain as prime minister for two terms, wrote
chiding his envoy Captain Charles Elliot for devoting energy to
gain a "barren island with hardly a House upon it" that had no
chance of ever being a great "Mart of Trade." As Chief Super-
intendent of British Trade in China, Elliot had taken a leading
role in the negotiations with officials of the Qing Dynasty over
the concessions those Manchu rulers needed to make as they
were going down in defeat to British forces in the First Opium
War. Palmerston's main reason for writing to Elliot, who had
recently secured British control of Hong Kong, was to tell him
his role as a negotiator had been so unsatisfactory that he would
be demoted. What Elliot secured, Palmerston thought, was not

26   a fitting victor's prize for Britain in the crucial Pearl River Delta
      region that was the central place for trade between the Qing and
      the West. Instead of claiming a port on par with Macau (a Por-
      tuguese colony whose importance in international commerce
      had been partially eclipsed by the rise of nearby Canton, aka
      Guangzhou, but was still a significant center of trade), the cap-
      tain had merely claimed a relatively insignificant island that was
      little known even within the southern part of the Qing Empire.
      "*All* we wanted might have been got, if it had not been for the
      unaccountably strange conduct of Charles Elliot," Queen Vic-
      toria complained in a letter, "who completely disobeyed his
      instructions and *tried* to get the *lowest* terms he could."

      Hong Kong Island was not quite as humble a spot as Palm-
      erston and Queen Victoria made it out to be, but it was at best
      a minor community at the time. One cause of the Opium War
      was frustration over the imperial court limiting all Western
      merchants other than the Portuguese to carrying out business
      exclusively through Canton, and only being able to go there at
      certain times of the year. To move the China trade forward in the
      way Palmerston felt necessary, Britain needed a suitable port of
      its own, and Hong Kong, not even thirty square miles in size,
      just would not fit the bill.

      Palmerston, of course, was completely wrong about Hong
      Kong's potential. The port soon proved a serious competitor
      to Macau and Canton for regional preeminence. It also grew
      dramatically in size. First, in 1860, after the Qing forces were
      bested by combined British and French forces (with some help
      from the Americans) in a Second Opium War, the colony added
      the Kowloon Peninsula, which stands across the harbor from
      Hong Kong Island and is roughly one-and-a-half times as big

as it in terms of square miles. Then, in 1898, the colony grew several-fold when the Qing ceded to Britain a tract of rural land located between Kowloon and the Shenzhen River, as well as a constellation of nearby islands. These additions—known collectively as the New Territories—included many villages and also Lantau Island, which is now home to the Hong Kong airport. The 1898 acquisitions gave the colony its final shape, but the New Territories were not given to Britain in perpetuity, as had been the case with Hong Kong Island and Kowloon. They were leased for ninety-nine years, which is why 1997 soon became a potential expiration date for the city's colonial period, especially given how dependent the populations of Hong Kong Island and Kowloon became on the New Territories for resources, including food and water.

By the time Hong Kong reached its final size, it had caught up with Macau and Canton as a "Mart of Trade," and it had far surpassed both as a financial center. It had also established a place for itself in the international imagination as a major port of call and was beginning to attract foreign tourists. Jules Verne had his adventurer Phileas Fogg make a stop in Hong Kong in *Around the World in Eighty Days*, comparing it to "a town in Kent or Surrey transferred by some strange magic to the antipodes." The Chinese traveler Li Gui, who visited Hong Kong at the start of an actual trip around the world, wrote that the harbor's merchant ships had "masts standing up like chopsticks" and that, at night, "lamps illuminate everything brilliantly with countless thousands of lights—a magnificent spectacle."

Shanghai also rocketed to importance after being opened to Western trade and settlement by the First Opium War. The city at the mouth of the Yangtze River, the longest in China,

28   was already a significant market town and transshipment port
      for goods bound for Southeast Asia well before the 1840s.
      Rather than being taken by Britain as a colony, it became at
      war's end one of a set of subdivided "treaty ports" that had both
      Qing-controlled parts and a district run by the British, with
      other foreign-run enclaves being added later to it. The city took
      on a tripartite form: a section that was part of China, an Inter-
      national Settlement run by a locally elected Municipal Council
      that was dominated by British and American interests initially
      and later became more robustly cosmopolitan, and a French
      Concession that was more like a miniature colony.

      Until the end of World War II, Hong Kong was in the shadow
      of Shanghai in most regards. Soon after the 1945 Japanese sur-
      render, though, they reversed positions. This was the result of,
      first, the threat of the Communist Party's conquest of Shanghai,
      and then the reality of Communist rule sending people, from
      fashion designers and filmmakers to merchants and mobsters,
      fleeing south to capitalist and colonial Hong Kong. During the
      Mao Zedong years (1949–1976), Shanghai became much less
      like Hong Kong and much less international, shedding most of
      its ties to Western countries, even as it maintained connections
      to other parts of the world, especially countries in the Soviet
      bloc. Shanghai did keep some distinctive reminders of its cos-
      mopolitan past, including the stunning architectural landmarks
      that line its waterfront Bund. Overall, though, it became much
      like other mainland cities and less a place that stood apart from
      them due to its greater connections to the wider world. When
      in 1923, the Hongkong and Shanghai Banking Corporation, or
      HSBC, today the largest bank in Europe, opened its neoclassical
      Shanghai branch on the Bund, it was the second largest bank

building in the world, and called "the most luxurious building
from the Suez Canal to the Bering Strait." But by 1955, HSBC had
shrunk its operations in Shanghai dramatically and was forced
to hand over the building to the Communists, who turned it into
offices for the municipal authorities.

Shanghai's fate after 1949 has always provided a model
for what could happen to Hong Kong after 1997. Some argued
in the mid-1990s that Hong Kong would be left alone by the
Communist Party after the Handover due to its economic
value, like the proverbial Golden Goose that needed to be cod-
dled so as to continue to lay precious eggs. Yet, Shanghai after
falling in 1949 was an example of a Golden Goose that the
Communists killed not long after taking control of it (though
it is perhaps now more like a Phoenix that has since risen
from the ashes and, after decades of recovery, competes with
Hong Kong for the title of China's premier financial hub in
many areas, even surpassing it in a few). There were some who
insisted in the early days of Communist rule that the fervently
anti-colonialist CCP would invade Hong Kong rather than try
to broker a transfer of control down the line when the lease of
the New Territories ended.

An invasion didn't happen, of course, and negotiating
the future of Hong Kong was exactly what the two sides had
to accomplish before the clock ticked midnight. In borrowed
space, on borrowed time—that was how Hong Kongers saw
their fate. So when it came time to determine the details of the
transfer of power, it fell to the British to get a good deal for Hong
Kong. After protracted negotiations, Prime Minister Margaret
Thatcher and Premier Zhao Ziyang signed the Sino-British
Joint Declaration on December 19, 1984, establishing the basic

30   ground rules for the city's future as an SAR. The agreement stip-
     ulated that Hong Kong after 1997 would enjoy "a high degree of
     autonomy" under "One Country, Two Systems," and that the
     Hong Kong way of life would remain largely unchanged for fifty
     years—setting up 2047 as another expiration date under a new
     period of borrowed time.

          The resulting constitution that was derived from the joint
     declaration also stipulated that the "ultimate aim" was to select
     Hong Kong's post-Handover governor, to be called "chief exec-
     utive," and members of the legislature, called the "Legislative
     Council" (LegCo, for short), by "universal suffrage." Unfortu-
     nately, nothing is said about how and when this "ultimate aim"
     would be achieved, and even more controversially, the final
     "interpretation" of the constitution would be done not by inde-
     pendent Hong Kong courts, but by the Standing Committee of
     China's legislature, the National People's Congress.

          The Hong Kong Basic Law was adopted with these gen-
     eral principles in place when Chinese president Yang Shangkun
     signed the constitution on April 4, 1990. But less than a year
     earlier, Yang, who initially seemed sympathetic to demands
     by student protesters in Beijing's Tiananmen Square, changed
     course and, along with other senior Communist Party leaders,
     condemned the demonstrations. His nephew even commanded
     an army unit during the June Fourth Massacre. With this
     frightful reminder, Hong Kongers were again asking: Is Hong
     Kong once more on the brink?

          "China will honor the commitments that she has made with
     us about the future of Hong Kong because I think she'll wish to
     be seen to honor them in the forum of the world," Thatcher told
     BBC listeners to a call-in show two months after the Basic Law

was ratified. Despite a question from one caller about how the events of 1989 would affect her perspective, Thatcher insisted that she still believed China's economic development would pave the way for democratic reform, and that Hong Kong's freedoms would be safe in the future. Six years had passed since she and paramount leader Deng Xiaoping had worked out their joint agreement, and there had been hope in the West that Deng's talk of "reform and opening" would lead to a liberalization of not just China's economy but also its political structures. This hope dissipated dramatically when the People's Liberation Army carried out the June Fourth Massacre. Deng's role in that state violence and the related acts of repression (such as a second massacre in Chengdu) that crushed the movement centered at Tiananmen Square engendered considerable doubt in the West about whether he deserved to be seen as a "liberalizer." This in turn sparked skepticism about his willingness to let Hong Kong go its own way for five decades after the Handover.

The events of 1989 also had a profound effect in Hong Kong itself. Even before the shooting started, there had been impressive local efforts to support the protesters at Tiananmen Square, including a benefit concert that helped raise money to buy supplies for activists in the north. (Sir Percy Cradock, Thatcher's ambassador to China, later said: "I recall that Jiang Zemin took me to the window of the Great Hall of the People, pointed out to the Square and said, there were the tents and they were put up with Hong Kong money.") The killings triggered a massive June march that was the largest gathering of its kind in the history of colonial Hong Kong. (There was also a big rally in Macau, involving an even larger percentage of that smaller community's population; an interesting point to remember, given

32   how much more tightly controlled and less prone to protest the
former Portuguese colony would be than the former British one
once both became SARs in the late 1990s.) Even many local residents who had been looking forward to 1997 as the year when
an unjust imperial system would end began to wonder whether
they had been too quick to assume that having Hong Kong
come under Chinese control would be a good thing if it involved
becoming part of a country run by people who had seemed ded-
icated reformers, but now were revealing hard-liner colors. For
those in Hong Kong who were already interested in gaining
greater democratic rights, the Handover in 1997 was a stain on
Britain akin to—although not as deadly as—the way in which
China's reputation had been shattered by the killings in 1989.

But Thatcher claimed that while she was concerned about
the brutal repressive moves the Communist Party had carried
out the previous year, she remained confident that the promises made in 1984 would be kept. She was convinced—or at least
claimed to be convinced—that Deng was a leader whose commitment to economic reform differentiated him sharply from
Mao. Despite the setbacks of 1989, she asserted that China was
on a general trajectory that would keep making it less and less
like the anti-capitalist and chaos-prone country it had been
decades before, when the mainland was roiled by a Cultural Revolution whose effects spilled over into the colony in the form of
Red Guard—inspired and Beijing-backed riots in 1967.

One could argue she was not completely wrong. Initially,
little was done to alter Hong Kong's capitalist economy, and
its civil society and legal system remained distinctive. In the
long run, though, she was far too sanguine, overestimating how
much appearances in the "forum of the world" would matter

to Deng's successors. (He died just before the Handover took place.) She also, perhaps, overestimated how much the "forum of the world" and Britain itself would stay attentive to Hong Kong's situation in the decades to come.

Thatcher was not alone in being optimistic as the Handover neared. Beijing official publications certainly claimed the same thing. Many businesspeople expected China's leaders to keep their promises, at least when it came to economic affairs. For example, according to an article titled "A City Bullish on Itself," which appeared in the March 1997 issue of *The Foreign Service Journal*, "more than 95 per cent of the 663 members" of the local American Chamber of Commerce who responded to a survey chose "favorable" or "very favorable" as their answer to a question asking how they expected the "city's business environment" to be during the next five years.

There were at least two reasons that China might refrain from meddling too much that had little to do with wishing to be seen by the "forum of the world" as being true to their word. Beijing had touted the "One Country, Two Systems" approach as something that in the future could be applied to Taiwan. Allowing a "high degree of autonomy" to Hong Kong might be helpful, one line of thinking went, in laying the groundwork for Beijing to claim a much bigger territorial prize down the road. Then there was the Golden Goose argument: Gaining prosperous Hong Kong would be an economic boon to China and it would be left largely as it was to ensure it remained an attractive locale for investors and companies.

Then, there were those who were far less optimistic. "Supposedly, Britain's handover in less than 750 days of Hong Kong, the world's most aggressively pro-business economy, to China,

34   the world's largest still officially communist dictatorship,
        is going to be a nonevent," Louis Kraar, former Asia editor of
        Fortune, wrote in 1995, in an essay that appeared as the cover
        story of the international editions of the magazine under the
        title "The Death of Hong Kong." "The naked truth about Hong
        Kong's future can be summed up in two words: It's over." He
        asserted, for example, that in the immediate wake of the Han-
        dover, Hong Kong would become a "captive colony of Beijing," be
        transformed into a "global backwater," and become "just another
        mainland city" in most ways. The article suggested that there
        would soon be no more freedom of speech or freedom of the
        press in Hong Kong than there was across the border in nearby
        cities such as Guangzhou and Shenzhen.

        Kraar was by no means the only Cassandra in the Western
        media. There were journalists who claimed that even ahead
        of the Handover the "bill of rights is being emasculated," and
        who foresaw a time near on the horizon when "a puppet gov-
        ernor" loyal to Beijing would be "installed," and insisted the CCP
        would "abolish the legislature" as soon as the territory became
        part of China. (Kraar and other journalists were not wrong
        about the legislature: China, furious that the last governor of
        Hong Kong, Chris Patten, had "unilaterally" reformed LegCo in
        1994 and held full elections for the body in 1995, set up a Provi-
        sional Legislative Council in Shenzhen, and after the Handover
        it immediately abolished Hong Kong's LegCo and installed the
        Provisional one until 1998.)

        Thatcher's optimism has proved problematic. There are
        many people who now feel that, even though we are well before
        the proposed 2047 expiration date for the "One Country, Two
        Systems" framework, Beijing has stopped honoring many of

its commitments. However, Kraar's pessimistic position was also off the mark. The Communist Party exerted a much lighter touch on Hong Kong immediately after the Handover than he predicted it would. In 2007, *Fortune* devoted a story exclusively to detailing the 1995 commentary's shortcomings, titled "Oops! Hong Kong is Hardly Dead." At least economically if not politically, China had "left Hong Kong alone to thrive" under its "One Country, Two Systems pledge." A variety of other articles have been published over the years that single out "The Death of Hong Kong" as an example of a faulty forecast, making it a rival to Palmerston's letter as the most oft-cited mistaken prediction about Hong Kong. But Kraar was also not completely wrong, and his biggest mistake, too, was timing—just in the opposite direction from Thatcher's. Some developments he worried about happening right away would only occur after many years had passed. He was not wrong to worry about elements of the city dying, just about how quickly they would expire.

One person who has had many reasons to be pessimistic since the Handover is Chris Patten, the last governor of Hong Kong. Loathed by Beijing, he has long been an excuse for China to trot out stories about British interference in general. Patten is called out specifically as someone who had tried to undermine the "One Country, Two Systems" arrangement before it went into effect, by expanding the political rights of local citizens after he took office in 1992. Patten introduced the reforms that made the Legislative Council basically elected through "universal suffrage" in 1995, and amended many restrictions on Hong Kongers' political liberties, including relaxing a draconian Public Order Ordinance from the 1960s that had, and would be, used to outlaw some of the city's largest demonstrations.

36   Beijing abolished Patten's elected legislature immediately after the Handover, and the Provisional Legislative Council rolled back Patten's reforms.

I met Patten—formally Lord Patten of Barnes, a leafy suburb in southwest London—in May of 2019, in his home. As an American whose view of British lords comes from period dramas, I thought that a butler might answer the door, but he greeted me instead, and we proceeded to have a lively and wide-ranging discussion touching on everything from our shared admiration for Orwell's dystopian fiction and le Carré's spy novels, to our shared worries about the directions that Xi Jinping and Donald Trump, as nationalistic strongman leaders, had been taking the People's Republic of China and the United States.

He told me that since his governorship had ended, he had been surprised many times by events in Hong Kong. I asked him to give me his reaction to a proposition that had formed in my mind: Historians of the future may well claim it was surprising both how light a touch the Chinese Communist Party used when dealing with Hong Kong in the immediate wake of 1997, and by how quickly Beijing tightened the screws on the city from the mid-2010s on. He pondered this for a moment, then nodded in assent. It was then that Lord Patten made a comment that has stuck with me more than anything that anyone else I have interviewed for this book has said: "When the snow starts melting, it melts quickly."

Victories

Experts asked to make a list of the five most influential Chinese writers of the last hundred years would disagree on many points, but most would accept that two very different people would need to be on it: *Little Red Book* author Mao Zedong and a Hong Kong novelist named Louis Cha. The latter's nom de plume, Jin Yong, is a household name in many ethnic Chinese households in disparate parts of the world, and from 1955 to 1972 he wrote fourteen exuberantly fantastical and epic works in the genre of *wuxia*, which chronicle martial arts heroes in tales of adventure in ancient China—think *Game of Thrones* set in actual historical settings like the War of the Roses. They were serialized in Hong Kong newspapers, including the prominent *Ming Pao*, which he cofounded. Six of his "novels" each consist of more than a million Chinese characters, or the equivalent of more than 700,000 English words, longer than the entire *Lord of the Rings* series. He is often called the Chinese Tolkien, and he sells about as well—estimates range between 100 to 300 million copies, making him by far the best-selling Chinese novelist

38   ever. His works have been adapted into countless movies, tele-
       vision shows, and video games. Cha died in Hong Kong at the
       age of ninety-four in 2018.

       Deng Xiaoping was a big fan of Cha's work, and in 1985, Cha
       was appointed to the fifty-nine-member committee (twenty-
       three from Hong Kong, thirty-six from the mainland, all chosen
       by Beijing, not jointly selected with London) that would draft
       the Basic Law of Hong Kong. Despite the fact that there were
       only two bona-fide liberals in the group, in 1988 the committee
       began formulating three proposals on how to elect the chief
       executive after the Handover, all of which would have guaran-
       teed universal suffrage by 2005. To the shock of many in Hong
       Kong, Cha introduced his own recommendation at the last
       minute, which was by far the most conservative of the four
       models: Universal suffrage would be determined by a refer-
       endum, but not until 2012 at the earliest. When the committee
       adopted Cha's model, activists held hunger strikes and burned
       copies of *Ming Pao*. Nevertheless, an even more ambiguous
       approach was written into Article 45 of the Basic Law, without
       even the guarantee of a 2012 referendum:

       > The method for selecting the Chief Executive shall be specified
       > in the light of the actual situation in the Hong Kong Special
       > Administrative Region and in accordance with the principle of
       > gradual and orderly progress. The ultimate aim is the selection
       > of the Chief Executive by universal suffrage upon nomination
       > by a broadly representative nominating committee in accor-
       > dance with democratic procedures.

       Since "the light of the actual situation" changes, the method
       then is fought over prior to every election. Whenever a new

chief executive is chosen, this is not done via an *election* but, as is made clear in Article 45, actually simply a *selection*. There is voting involved (as there tends to be even for the leadership of China's Communist Party), but only a very small number of people get to participate—400 in the 1996 "Selection Committee," gradually increasing to 1,194 in the 2012 and 2017 "Election Committees." And they only get to choose among limited options. In the case of selecting a new General Secretary for the Party, the pretense of a democratic process is hard to take seriously: Only a handful of people vote and sometimes there is just one choice. In the Hong Kong case, things have been less tightly controlled and there are people—usually three—who run against each other for the chief executive spot. Still, fewer than 1,200 Hong Kong residents serve as electors, and they have to choose among candidates who have been carefully vetted to ensure that the winner will be someone acceptable to Beijing.

It is difficult to overstate how strange and enigmatic the Basic Law of Hong Kong is. By stipulating that elections will be "specified in the light of the actual situation," it is as if Beijing has dared its small territory to the south to constantly and never-endingly fight for every inch of political self-determination. One thinks of a parent (Hong Kongers derisively call Beijing leaders their "grandfathers") who drives a child crazy by promising candy that he never delivers. And that's exactly what has occurred ever since the Handover. Every political battle has had to do with Beijing gaslighting on universal suffrage, even if the massive protests in 2003 and 2012 have been ostensibly about something else. Democracy is and always has been the dominant issue in Hong Kong politics.

In the summer of 2003, hundreds of thousands of Hong Kong residents spilled out into the streets to protest a proposed security bill designed to ensure that the local government would be able to vigorously stamp out all signs of "sedition" in the territory. Those backing the bill insisted it was nothing more than carrying out Article 23 of the Basic Law, which stipulated that the local authorities would in due time introduce rules relating to the steps that could be taken to ensure that the former colony remained free of turbulence:

> The Hong Kong Special Administrative Region shall enact laws on its own to prohibit any act of treason, secession, sedition, subversion against the Central People's Government, or theft of state secrets, to prohibit foreign political organisations or bodies from conducting political activities in the Region, and to prohibit political organisations or bodies of the Region from establishing ties with foreign political organisations or bodies.

At one level, the bill was straightforward enough. It had elements in it not all that different from the "Patriot Act" that had been implemented in the United States in the aftermath of 9/11. The government of Hong Kong's first chief executive, Tung Chee-hwa, the son of a Chinese shipping tycoon and a pro-Beijing loyalist, presented it as simply fulfilling the terms of the constitution. But the timing and precise wording of the final version was significant. As Danny Gittings, a journalist and legal scholar based at the University of Hong Kong, stresses in his *Introduction to the Basic Law,* the definitive book on the topic, a version of Article 23 heading toward approval before the Tiananmen crisis of 1989 had not included the reference to "subversion" and concern with "foreign political organisations." Those were added after they became terms Beijing used in its efforts to present its use of force against unarmed protesters in June 1989 as a justified move to stop what it claimed were Western-backed efforts to overthrow the Communist Party.

When the local authorities spelled out how exactly subversion would be criminalized in Hong Kong, at a time when groups such as the Falun Gong sect that were persecuted across the mainland were able to pass out materials on street corners, there was bound to be controversy. What government backers of Article 23 failed to predict was how widespread the anger at the bill would be. Opposition was not limited to those, such as Falun Gong sectarians, who were involved in actions that they had good reason to think would be criminalized if the proposed Article 23 bill went into effect. Many thousands of locals came to feel that the bill's implementation would lead to the disappearance of key features of local life. A groundswell of opposition to the bill grew, and on the sixth anniversary of the Handover, more than half a million people took part in a July 1 "anti-Article 23" rally at Victoria Park. This gathering, the largest protest the city had seen since 1989, was the first in a dramatic series of interrelated but distinctive popular expressions of discontent that would sporadically rock the city over the course of the next dozen years.

The government eventually reversed course on implementing its Article 23 plan. This was a signal of victory for activists, a proof of the potential power of the people, even if periodically since then, the authorities have said or hinted that they may revive the plan or present a similar one. As local scholar Suzanne Pepper often stresses in her work, this is a

42   perpetual threat to whatever degree of autonomy Hong Kong
      continues to have at any given time. Tung was exactly one year
      into his second five-year term as chief executive when the July
      demonstration took place, and it was one of several factors that
      led Tung to step down in 2005, becoming the first but by no
      means the last chief executive to fail to serve the ten years in
      power that Beijing hoped would be standard for the post.

      Politics was not the only factor that led to Tung's resig-
      nation. The degree of inequality in the territory is staggering.
      While 18 percent of Hong Kongers lived under the poverty line
      in 2016, the net worth of Hong Kong's top ten billionaires repre-
      sented 35 percent of the city's GDP, compared to 3 percent in the
      U.S. Hong Kong's Gini coefficient, a measurement of income
      distribution, is one of the highest in the world at 0.533.

      The economy of Hong Kong had stalled over the course of
      Tung's term, though it wasn't all his fault. The day after the
      Handover, the Asian financial crisis began, when Thailand's
      government devalued its currency, the baht, which led investors
      to pull their money out of the country and the region, leading
      to a chain reaction that brought down stock markets all across
      East Asia, including the largest one, the Hong Kong Stock
      Exchange. For the first time since World War II, Hong Kong's
      gross domestic product shrank, by almost 6 percent, in 1998.

      All of this came as quite a shock to Hong Kong, whose
      baby-boom generation had seen nothing but remarkable
      growth for most of their lives. (The GDP had risen by 9 percent
      in the 1970s and 7.4 percent in the 1980s. Since the Handover,
      it has dropped to about 3 percent, lagging behind competitors
      such as Singapore and Taiwan.) Unemployment rose to nearly
      9 percent by 2003. Property prices during the financial crisis

fell more than 60 percent, and families suddenly found their
homes worth less than the outstanding balance on their mort-
gage loans—what's called "negative equity," which was widespread at the time.

An older generation of Hong Kongers had seen prosperity
thanks to hitching their ride to China's booming economy, but
around this time the number of Hong Kong companies oper-
ating in China began to drop, as the territory was losing its role
as the gateway to the mainland. Baby boomers believed that the
way to restore Hong Kong's centrality was to follow China's lead,
but to a younger generation that never fully benefited from Hong
Kong's postwar miracle, that was not the answer. Youth unemployment rose to an all-time high of 10.4 percent in August
2003. Average wages were flat for a decade after the Handover.
Young Hong Kongers saw their future as increasingly grim.

Myriad factors may have contributed to Hong Kongers'
malaise, but the most important issue for many remained the
question of how light or heavy Beijing's hand would be in the
future, how much of the promised autonomy the SAR would
be able to retain. So when Tung's successor as chief executive,
the longtime civil servant Donald Tsang, announced plans for
an upheaval of the curriculum in Hong Kong's schools in 2010,
it was met with skepticism and even anger. Specifically, the
new curriculum would redouble the emphasis on "moral and
national education," intended to shape Hong Kong's schoolchil-
dren into loyal citizens of the PRC. The new curriculum would
flatter the CCP, in part by effacing any references to what had
happened in Tiananmen Square roughly two decades prior.

In 2011, a group of Hong Kong students converged under
the name Scholarism to publicly oppose the moral and national

44   education plan. Led by the bespectacled Joshua Wong—who was then not yet fifteen and who would emerge as the face of much larger civic unrest three years later—Scholarism's members, Agnes Chow among them, had mostly been infants at the time of the 1997 Handover. They demanded the rights they said had been bequeathed to their generation in the language of the Basic Law, which pledged a "high degree of autonomy" to Hong Kong. In the summer of 2012, Scholarism and those sympathetic to its concerns marched across the city. Turnout was estimated at just shy of 100,000. In August dozens of them occupied Hong Kong's government headquarters for more than a week. The government announced on September 8 that it would suspend consideration of the moral and national education reform, but the protests had uncorked something greater. A new generation of Hong Kongers had learned that they could speak out for the democratic values they considered their birthright.

After pro-Beijing politician Leung Chun-ying was "elected" as chief executive in 2012, activists began clamoring for a change via an "Occupy" movement. They pointed out that Beijing had assured Hong Kongers before 1997 that they would eventually be able to choose who was in charge of their city, something they had been unable to do under the colonial system. There had been failed efforts to make the selection of the chief executive more democratic in 2007. Now there was a push to see a popular vote for this position in 2017, a symbolically resonant point in time, as twenty years would have passed since the Handover. There were calls as well to make the Legislative Council more truly democratic by 2020. (There have long been key features of LegCo that limit the degree it reflects popular sentiments—and

prevents pro-democracy, anti-Beijing members, who have his-   45
torically garnered the support of more than half of Hong Kong
voters, from ever obtaining a majority in the legislature. Only
half of LegCo is directly elected by the people of Hong Kong.
Thirty-five seats are reserved for "geographical constituencies"; that is, they are elected to office, by districts, via an
openly contested voting process that involves campaigns and
parties of the sort that residents of countries such as the United
States and the United Kingdom would recognize. But the other
half of the seats have been set aside for "functional constituencies," a bizarre system made up of occupational and interest
groups, including "financial services" and "real estate and con-
struction." Accountants are allotted one of the thirty-five seats,
and so are caterers. Worse yet, as if the U.S. Supreme Court's
Citizens United v. FEC decision has been taken to the extreme,
corporations actually get to vote for these seats. The "finance"
legislator—different from the "financial services" one—is
determined by just 125 financial companies and organizations,
in fact, by the executives of these bodies. One can be excused for
failing to understand why 141 insurance CEOs' vastly outsized
political votes are somehow essential to the governance of Hong
Kong. Functional constituencies are in place solely to allow Beijing to choose representatives acceptable to them, and who are
ready to back the policies of the Communist Party. Functional
constituency "elections" are a farce, since often one candidate
has basically been given the seat via an under-the-table deal.
This system was and still is a colonial one. It was created by the
last masters to limit democracy and adopted and adapted hap-
pily by the current ones. Pro-Beijing members have historically dominated the functional constituency half of LegCo, to

46   the tune of twenty-four seats in the last elections in 2016, compared to only ten seats held by the anti-Beijing camp.)

The main initiator of Occupy Central with Love and Peace
was Benny Tai, a member of the University of Hong Kong's law
faculty. He insisted at the start of 2013 that there had been a
breach of faith on the side of the political establishment and that
a bold act of civil disobedience was needed to overcome it and
to push for democracy in Hong Kong. The territory had become
a bit more democratic during the final years of British rule, as
Chris Patten, without London's blessing or approval, strove to
provide the populace with added protections before the territory was incorporated into China. Hong Kong was supposed
to become more democratic still after 1997, but right after the
Handover, some moves that Patten had made were reversed and
promises for new reforms were watered down and delayed. By
the early 2010s, moves toward true representation had stalled
completely; without popular pressure being applied, the 2017
chief executive would be chosen in much the same way as previous ones. There was talk of expanding the number of people
who could vote while keeping the vetting of candidates, but that
seemed to Tai and his allies like a cosmetic change that would
not solve the fundamental issue. There were just two main differences between the old governor system and the new chief
executive one, in their view: People of Chinese descent now held
the top spot, and the person on top was beholden to a different
far-off capital, Beijing rather than London.

The problem of how chief executives were chosen was com-
pounded, in the eyes of Hong Kong progressives, by the Legislative Council situation. There were oppositional political
parties known collectively as constituting a "pan-democratic"

coalition, but the best members of it could hope to do in most cases—and then only if they allied tightly with one another (there were often divisions among them)—was delay or block laws limiting freedom. They were stymied when it came to finding strategies to proactively extend liberties. Like the limited advisory role given to members of Hong Kong's Chinese elite during parts of the colonial era, locals were unable to control their own fate. For all the talk of an era of domination by outside forces ending in 1997, Tai and other critics argued, Hong Kong was still effectively under external control, just via different proxies and different mechanisms.

It was against this backdrop that calls for a change in the chief executive selection process gained steam throughout 2013 and during the spring and early summer of 2014. A compromise approach was floated, which would introduce universal suffrage but again keep the vetting process in place, but this was rejected by Tai and others calling for an Occupy movement, such as Chan Kin-man, a Chinese University of Hong Kong sociologist who became Tai's closest collaborator in the effort.

The original name for the 2014 movement linked Hong Kong's struggle for democracy to contemporaneous Occupy movements. The tie to Occupy Wall Street was especially clear. Hong Kong's financial district is nearest to the "Central" and "Admiralty" MTR stations, and Tai and his colleagues combined a concern with increasing democratic procedures in Hong Kong with a criticism of the large and rapidly increasing economic divide in the city between the very wealthy and everyone else. These were intertwined issues, since the chief executives tended to be drawn from—or at least show a proven ability to ally with—a small cohort of rich developers who comprise

48   Hong Kong's business elite. The added final words in the move-
      ment's name, "With Love and Peace," flagged the fact that some
      key organizers of the drive were people of faith who drew inspi-
      ration from both famous Christian proponents of nonviolence,
      such as Martin Luther King Jr., and non-Christian civil disobe-
      dience heroes, such as Gandhi.

      The Occupy Central plan almost failed to materialize, as
      Tai grew dispirited by late summer about its prospects for suc-
      cess and became disappointed by the lack of unity among pro-
      democracy forces in Hong Kong. Students, however, stepped
      in—both those of Joshua Wong and Agnes Chow's generation
      and others who were in their twenties and, in some cases, had
      been involved in environmental protests before 2012 as well as
      in the fight to block the importing of patriotic education. In the
      middle of September—after anger was sparked by the Standing
      Committee of the National People Congress's August 31 "deci-
      sion" on Hong Kong's methods for choosing chief executives,
      which made it clear that the CCP was determined to block all
      moves toward genuine universal suffrage in the territory—the
      students launched a classroom strike. Then, after there were
      revived calls for an Occupy movement to begin in October,
      activists much younger than Tai and Chan jumped the gun and
      began holding rallies by government buildings and sleeping on
      the streets.

      The original middle-aged and older leaders of Occupy Cen-
      tral—Tai and Chan were often described as part of a trio whose
      third member was Reverend Chu Yiu-ming, a Baptist preacher
      in his seventies—scrambled to keep from getting left behind by
      these developments. They remained important figures in the
      struggle. Increasingly, though, they had to share the limelight

with and often cede agenda setting to younger activists, who
sometimes found inspiration in the same places (e.g., Wong,
like Tai and Chu, routinely describes his activism as rooted in
his Christianity) but sometimes in other places. For example,
the Sunflower Movement that had taken place in Taiwan earlier
in 2014, during which activists concerned with growing mainland influence in their country had staged an occupation of the
national legislature, was an important point of reference for
Hong Kong activists who were in their teens and twenties.

The emergence of a second set of leaders, made up of teens
like Wong and Chow and a set of youths in their twenties
involved in the very influential at the time Hong Kong Federation of Students, was matched by an increasing tendency to use
a second name, Umbrella Movement, or sometimes Umbrella
Revolution, for the struggle. They also often struck a more confrontational tone in addressing the Hong Kong government.
Many of the younger protesters were in step with international
currents. This showed through in the eclectic symbolism they
drew on in protest art that mixed nods to China's past with nods
to global youth culture figures such as the insurgents of the *V for
Vendetta* series. But the Umbrella Movement name was a more
locally rooted one than Occupy Central. It was derived from the
implement, so ubiquitous in rainy Hong Kong, that activists
used to shield their faces during standoffs with police who used
first pepper spray and then tear gas against protesters.

The use of tear gas on September 28 was especially conse-
quential. Images of groups of people using umbrellas to block its
effect and a photograph of a lone man holding an umbrella while
clouds of gas swirled around him became iconic shots seen
around the world. There was even for a time a sculpture inspired

50   by the photograph of the lone man that seemed as though it might have the kind of impact and longevity as a symbol that the Goddess of Democracy and the Tank Man had in 1989, though it ended up having a much shorter half-life as an iconic image.

Local police had deployed tear gas before in post-Handover Hong Kong, during a wave of anti-WTO protests in 2005. This had shocked people at the time. The targets of the police measures then, though, had largely been people from other places, especially farmers who had come over from South Korea to try to disrupt the international gathering. According to many reports, and not just official sources or periodicals that tended to sympathize with the police, the WTO protesters had been using militant tactics and ratcheting up tensions before the tear gas was used. For example, the demonstrators had, according to the *Guardian,* wielded "iron bars, wooden poles, and battering rams," and both sides took extreme measures during a day that saw Hong Kong roiled by the "most violent street clashes in more than 30 years," creating the sort of turmoil on the streets that had been unknown in that "normally sedate commercial city . . . since the 1960s." The use of tear gas in 2005, however, was widely seen as a one-off response to special circumstances (in which those harmed by it were mostly working-class protesters from another country as opposed to Hong Kong students), and it had not become a standard part of the repertoire of repression. To have it used against unarmed Hong Kongers, most of them young, some known to be from leading local universities, outraged a broad spectrum of the populace. It instantly turned many people who had been passive observers of the movement into strong sympathizers and in some cases

active participants in it. It is sometimes hard to remember now
how surprising its deployment then was, given that countless
volleys would be fired during the middle months of 2019.

The symbolism of umbrellas also has added meaning in
Hong Kong due to the main character that refers to the implement in Cantonese. The first character in the name Chater Road,
which runs near the Admiralty MTR station and was where
some major protests took place in 2014 and in other years, also
means umbrella. This character also conveys a sense of pro-
tecting oneself while striking back. The militant implications
of the term fit with the style of youthful activists who—while
sharing many of the same values of Tai and Chan, such as a commitment to nonviolence and, especially in Wong's case, seeing
their activism as rooted in their faith—were readier to lash out
against those in power rhetorically and less patient in their
approach more generally.

It is easy to see impatience as linked to a timeless difference
between younger and older generations, but there is a better
explanation. If Chan Kin-man lives until 2047, he will be almost
ninety when the official end of the "One Country, Two Systems"
framework arrives. Agnes Chow will be in her early fifties. Chow
could well live for decades in whatever kind of city Hong Kong
becomes at that point, giving an urgency to her desire to make
sure the features of local life she prizes do not deteriorate mark-
edly before then. It also may make a difference that people of
Wong and Chow's age never had the experience that some ethnically Chinese veterans of the 2003 protests had: of feeling like
second-class citizens in a British colony and looking forward
to seeing foreign rule end, as they were just toddlers or not yet

52   born when the Handover took place. For the younger genera-
      tion, Beijing has always been the capital that is most important
      and has the leaders most worth worrying about.

          Another experience that the Wong and Chow generation of
      protestors lacked, but which the 2003 veterans took seriously,
      was the memory of 1989. This goes some way to explaining why
      the Umbrella leaders seemed more determined to stay on the
      streets in the face of police aggression. Tai, Chan, and other
      activists their ages and older had all followed closely, in real
      time, the coverage of the terrible events that took place at the
      end of the Tiananmen movement when the Communist Party
      ordered its army to fire on the people of the People's Republic.
      Some of them, such as the Reverend Chu, had been active in
      efforts to aid Tiananmen Square protesters before the June
      Fourth Massacre and after that contributed to Operation Yellow
      Bird, a plan that tried, often with success, to help activists on
      Beijing's most wanted list reach safety by crossing the border
      into Hong Kong. Several years after the Occupy Movement, Tai
      wrote in the *Journal of Democracy* that he and those he worked
      most closely with in 2014 had "seen how the Tiananmen Mas-
      sacre happened." He continued as follows: "The souls of Tian-
      anmen Square have remained in our hearts, and never far from
      our thoughts. . . . Haunted by the nightmare of the Tiananmen
      Massacre, [we] just wanted to bring everyone home safely [after
      the police started to use tear gas against protestors]."

          In hindsight, it is easy to claim that all talk of a possible
      Hong Kong variant on Tiananmen in 2014 was hyperbolic.
      There was never a serious possibility then that the Party would
      use lethal force against protesters. There were several checks
      on such actions. One was the amount of global attention the

Umbrella Movement was getting. Another was the fact that, in name at least, Hong Kongers were supposed to enjoy the freedom to protest. A third, whose significance should not be understated, was that a key fear of the Party has long been of movements that affect multiple locales and involve large numbers of people from many different classes. The Tiananmen movement, though associated above all with gatherings at one plaza, saw large-scale demonstrations occur in scores of cities. But there were no major sympathy protests on the mainland while the Umbrella Movement was underway, and there was always a sense that participation in 2014 event was primarily the work of specific segments of the local populace, albeit ones that had the sympathy of many different sorts of Hong Kongers. Finally, the Umbrella Movement only affected a few locations within Hong Kong. There were, in other words, some important contrasts not just with the Tiananmen movement but also with the events of 2019, which have involved much larger crowds, had more demonstrations drawing attention to the support for the struggle by varied classes, and played out across a much wider geographical terrain within Hong Kong—though, again, without triggering sympathy protests across the border on the mainland or even in Macau, which is also a Special Administrative Region and a place where June Fourth vigils are held (albeit small ones).

Even though the fear of a June Fourth—style massacre taking place in 2014 now seems misplaced, it is easy to understand why Tai's generation and their elders viewed this as a real possibility. It makes sense that they would view it in any case as a more plausible potential outcome of activism than did youths like Wong, who fought for the right to be taught about

54   the June 4th Massacre, but could not as easily imagine a repeat
      of it taking place in their city.

      There were also specific economic issues that stood out for
the younger generation of 2014 activists. They were coming of
age at a time defined by skyrocketing housing costs and dimin-
ishing job prospects. As passionate in their attachment to Hong
Kong as their elders, even those who were studying at or might
have a chance soon to enter a top-tier local academic institution did not feel confident about being able to secure a job in
the future that would allow them to live a life of material com-
fort in the city they loved. To have a say in how this city was
run—or at least not see its civil liberties decay—was a matter
of special urgency, something that could help make up for economic difficulties.

      In the end, however, even weeks of dramatic street protests
in the fall of 2014 failed to alter political procedures. Despite
signs of widespread support in Hong Kong for an expansion of
democracy, the authorities stayed committed to keeping in place
a system that guaranteed that the next chief executive would be
someone acceptable to both Beijing and the local developers and
tycoons of Chinese descent with whom the Communist Party
had established a cozy relationship during the lead-up to the
Handover that grew even closer after 1997. (There were excep-
tions within this segment of the Hong Kong business community, but on the whole, its members were less concerned about
Beijing's interference in local affairs than were many within the
international business community.) The result was that when
Carrie Lam rose to the post of chief executive in 2017, while it
was a novelty to have a woman assume that role and she came
from the ranks of the government bureaucracy rather than being

a leading tycoon as some of her predecessors had been, there
was something all-too-familiar about how she made it to the
top. She was chosen in the exact same way as those who preceded her to the post.

When I arrived in Hong Kong in early November of 2014,
there was a heady feeling among the protesters I met in the main
Occupy zone in Admiralty that they had accomplished something
simply by seizing and keeping control of the streets. The same
was true when I talked to people in Mong Kok, a working-class
district on the Kowloon side of the harbor where there was
another encampment. This was true even though, by that point,
people sleeping on the streets of Mong Kok had been attacked
by thugs, and even though, by that point, some people in each of
the two Occupy areas I visited (I did not make it to a third one,
in the shopping district of Causeway Bay on Hong Kong Island)
had been involved in scuffles with the police and in some cases
felt their eyes burn after pepper spray or tear gas volleys.

There had been no upsurge in any part of the People's
Republic during the twenty-five years following the June Fourth
Massacre of 1989 during which large crowds had kept gathering
in urban districts for weeks on end. The 2014 struggle was the
first to take place in the country in a quarter century that had
proved able to garner international media attention in more
than a transitory way. Joshua Wong had even been featured on
the cover of *TIME*. Not just his face, but those of other young
activists, such as his close comrade in arms Agnes Chow, had
appeared in news broadcasts seen everywhere from Vancouver
to Venezuela, Seoul to San Francisco. It made sense that I found
people on the streets who felt emboldened and energized by a
belief that they were part of something important, something

56   that had captured the imagination even of people living far from Hong Kong.

By that point, it seemed unlikely that they would make any headway on the specific issue of how the next chief executive would be chosen, but many still felt they had succeeded in making their views known. There had even been a dialogue between protest leaders (such as Hong Kong Federation of Students leaders Yvonne Leung, Nathan Law, and Alex Chow) and government officials that had been broadcast live on October 21. There were still other markers of success as well, which made the Umbrella Movement seem, for a time, like the third and perhaps greatest protest victory of the post-Handover period. One thing that meant a lot to activists was the expressions of support for their cause that came from local celebrities they admired, ranging from locally and regionally prominent Cantopop singers, such as Denise Ho, to the globally renowned actor Chow Yun-fat.

The Umbrella Movement became over time, as so many events of its kind become, a fight to defend the right to protest as much as anything else. That was a fight that many felt they were winning or indeed by early November had won. They had won, in the eyes of some, simply by standing their ground and transforming parts of Hong Kong into communal spaces suffused with something they felt was beautiful.

Punishments

For seventy-nine days at the end of 2014, the world watched as the Umbrella Movement brought Hong Kong to a standstill, metaphorically and at times literally. At its largest, the number of demonstrators assembled in the heart of the central business district and elsewhere in the city surpassed 100,000, disrupting the flow of life and commerce in one of the world's most vital economic centers and occasionally escalating into violent confrontations with police and counter-protesters. The city's busiest thoroughfares became communal campsites, where for nearly three months Hong Kongers of all ages and stripes assembled to petition for the democratic rights denied to them.

The protests finally subsided in mid-December, several weeks after the government issued formal injunctions on behalf of the city's taxi and minibus companies to clear the streets the demonstrators had occupied. But it was the fatigue of the protesters themselves, rather than any government decree, that ultimately returned Hong Kong to normalcy, however temporarily. The foremost demand of the Umbrella Movement—the

58   right to directly elect the chief executive by "universal suf-
       frage"—had gone unanswered by the government. Neverthe-
       less, the city's political fabric had changed inalterably. The
       mass protests had galvanized a generation of young Hong
       Kongers, awakening them to the political realities of life in the
       semi-autonomous territory and the ways they could fight for
       their futures. For the governments in Hong Kong and Beijing,
       the ideal means of subduing this discontent was suppressing
       it. In the months and years that followed, the state exercised
       tactics of legal and political force that were largely unprece-
       dented in Hong Kong but deeply familiar in the mainland—
       reinforcing Hong Kongers' anxiety that Beijing was effacing
       the distinctions between their home and the country to which
       it returned in 1997.
           Over the course of the first nine months of 2015, Joshua
       Wong was arrested and detained for three hours; accused by a
       local pro-Beijing newspaper of having CIA ties; blocked from
       entering Malaysia—and in 2016 Thailand—on the basis that
       his presence would hurt the country's relationship to China;
       and hassled by pro-Beijing "protesters" in the Taipei airport—
       these men, who had ties to local gangsters, threatened him,
       called him "independence scum," and told him he had no busi-
       ness being in Taiwan.
           Late in 2015, five Hong Kong booksellers disappeared—
       kidnapped and arrested by mainland Chinese authorities, it
       turns out—and then, in some cases, reappeared on television
       screens making confessions under duress after they had been
       imprisoned without access to lawyers.
           In February 2016, a conflict broke out in Mong Kok, which
       was called the "Fishball Riot" by some, the "Fishball Revolution"

by others. In the wake of this event, several activists who had
taken leadership roles in what were increasingly referred to as
"localist" movements were arrested. The focus of these movements was defending symbols of local identity: In 2006, activists held sit-ins to protest the demolition of the Star Ferry Pier, a
waterfront landmark; in 2007, they fiercely opposed the redevel-
opment of Hong Kong's famed Wedding Card Street into luxury
shopping and housing complexes; and in 2016, they opposed the
government's crackdown on unlicensed street hawkers—many
of whom sell fishballs, a popular Hong Kong street food. During
the Lunar New Year festivities, many hawkers were intimidated
and attacked by masked men and thugs. Protesters who came
to their rescue clashed with riot police, who arrested sixty-one
people and allegedly attacked and injured not only activists but
also journalists. One leading localist, Edward Leung, was later
sentenced to six years in jail on riot charges.

In June 2016, the French cosmetics house Lancôme, bowing
to pressure from Beijing, cut ties with the Cantopop singer
Denise Ho, who had been the face of the company's L'Oréal products in Hong Kong and the mainland even after she came out
as a lesbian at a 2012 gay pride parade and concert and became
active in LGBT causes. When the tear gassing of protesters in
late September 2014 outraged her and she joined the Umbrella
Movement, the Communist Party banned her from performing
and selling her music on the mainland, which, being a far larger
market than Hong Kong, is what most Cantopop stars rely on for
their livelihood. She has since become a staunch pro-democracy
activist. When in May 2016 she met with the Dalai Lama, Beijing branded her a separatist and gave Lancôme an ultimatum:
Cut ties with Ho or stop being able to market their products on

60   the mainland. The company took her face off billboards in Hong Kong and abruptly canceled plans for a concert of hers they were sponsoring.

On July 21, 2016, Joshua Wong was convicted of participating in an illegal assembly and on August 15 he was sentenced to perform eighty hours of community service. (This was for climbing over a fence near the LegCo building during a 2014 protest.) The Hong Kong government complained that the punishment was too light, appealed the case, and the sentence swelled to six months in prison.

On July 1, 2017, China's paramount leader Xi Jinping came to Hong Kong and gave a hard-line speech to mark the twentieth anniversary of the Handover that was broadcast widely in the territory and across the mainland. He made it crystal clear to listeners that he viewed the first two words in the "One Country, Two Systems" formulation to be the key ones, the second pair of much less importance, little more than an inconvenient leftover from a time when Beijing had been too weak to demand full control over the territory. While in Hong Kong, he also presided over what was by far the biggest display of troops and military hardware ever put on view within the territory.

Late in 2018, the West Kowloon station of the Express Rail Link opened, with parts of the station considered mainland Chinese territory and governed by mainland Chinese laws, instead of Hong Kong laws. Months later, the localist Hong Kong National Party was outlawed for promoting local independence, the first time that a political organization had been banned in this manner in Hong Kong. In the fall, *Financial Times* editor Victor Mallet was prevented from reentering Hong Kong after taking a trip, and his visa extension was denied with no

explanation for the move given, which is just what happens
when such things occur, as they periodically have for years, on
the mainland. This was likely a retaliation because Mallet had
moderated a Foreign Correspondents Club event that featured
the head of the Hong Kong National Party. In early November of
2018, an exhibition of work by Badiucao, a Chinese artist living
in exile in Australia, who was known for cartoons that mocked
Xi Jinping, was canceled at the last minute. (It was supposed to
take place at Hive Spring in the Aberdeen section of Hong Kong
Island, as part of a "free expression week" slate of activities.)
Then, days later, a venue with links to the local government
announced that it was reversing the earlier decision it had made
to host a Hong Kong International Literary Festival event featuring Chinese dissident novelist Ma Jian. The venue relented
and allowed the event to take place, after extracting a promise
from the Festival and from Ma Jian—who later revealed that no
Hong Kong publisher was willing to release his latest novel, a
work that has been described as presenting China under Xi as
a Big Brother state par excellence—that the focus of the event
would be on artistic issues as opposed to politics.

What was becoming very clear was that China was increasingly running the show in Hong Kong. The city has always had
staunchly democratic politicians, including a lawmaker nicknamed Long Hair who made a habit of heckling pro-Beijing government officials while draped in a Hong Kong flag, and another
nicknamed Mad Dog who threw a glass of water at C. Y. Leung.
But until 2016, Beijing had never before interfered in the governance of Hong Kong to the point of preventing a directly elected
legislator from taking his or her seat in the Legislative Council

62   chambers. This is just what it did, however, right after the first major post–Umbrella Movement election.

In April 2016, Joshua Wong and Agnes Chow joined with other activists to establish a new political party. They called it "Demosistō," and the initial goal of this successor to Scholarism was to get two of its members elected to the Legislative Council. One of the party's candidates, Oscar Lai, suspended his run due to lack of funds. The other, Nathan Law, won his race. At twenty-three, he became the youngest legislator in Hong Kong history. Overall, pro-democracy candidates did well in the 2016 elections, in which a record number of local registered voters went to the polls. Though the Hong Kong people only directly vote for half of the seventy-member LegCo, while the other half is made up of the bizarre "functional constituencies," nevertheless the anti-Beijing camp, which consists of traditional democrats as well as new localist cohorts, increased their majority in the directly elected seats to nineteen, compared to sixteen seats held by the pro-Beijing camp. The pro-democracy parties won about 1.2 million votes, compared to about 870,000 for the pro-Beijing parties. Even with the pro-Beijing dominance over the favorably designed functional constituency-half of LegCo, pro-democracy lawmakers still won twenty-nine of seventy seats, giving them a veto power on any reforms and amendments to Hong Kong's constitution (which required a two-thirds majority vote).

Law, who had become active in campus politics in 2013 and been a key player in the citywide protests in 2014, seemed in a good position going forward, as he had potential allies among some members of traditional parties and also among some other upstarts who had ridden the same post-Umbrella wave to victory. One thing that Law had in common with some other newly elected candidates in their twenties and thirties was a conviction that Hong Kong needed to fight to protect its rights to "self-determination" moving forward. One place there were fissures within the group was on whether they tried hard, as Law did, to make it clear that they were not calling for Hong Kong's "independence"—a term that may not seem that far removed from "self-determination" but was in the local context. (In a 2016 interview with Nash Jenkins of *TIME*, for example, Law stressed that what he sought for Hong Kong was not to have it become its own country but to gain "high autonomy, a fair political system, and social justice.") Hong Kong's government, taking its lead from cues sent by Beijing, insisted that any talk of "independence" violated the "One Country, Two Systems" and crossed a "red line"—a term Xi would use in his Handover anniversary speech. To even raise the possibility that Hong Kong might do better as an "independent" entity or a place with "self-rule" was, in the eyes of the authorities, to move out of the realm of acceptable political speech and into the domain of treason.

Another divide within the new cohort that Law was a part of had to do with how they took the standard oath of office. They were all eager to signal their outsider status by taking liberties with the oathtaking. Some opted for subtle variations to the protocol, such as slowing their speech down a bit, or making a statement about needing to preserve Hong Kong liberties before or after saying the required words, as a way to show that they had not completely left their roles as protesters behind. Law took this path. Others, though, chose more confrontational and dramatic forms of political theater.

64   Most notably, Sixtus Leung and Yau Wai-ching, who were respectively the most prominent male and female figures in Youngspiration, which like Demosistō had emerged from the Umbrella Movement but had leaders much fonder of confrontational tactics and less cautious than Wong and Law when speaking about issues associated with independence, went all out in mocking the ceremony. They draped themselves with a flag that read "Hong Kong is NOT China" and swore allegiance to the "Hong Kong nation"—a phrase that placed them on the wrong side of the "red line" in the eyes of both the local authorities and Beijing. They were immediately barred from taking their seats, but they appealed this decision—asking either that it be overturned completely or at least they be allowed to retake the oath. The issue was considered one for Hong Kong's judicial system to decide. Many assumed that the court would uphold their dismissal and might not allow them to take the oath a second time, but it was seen as an important marker of Hong Kong's "high degree of autonomy" and concern for the rule of law that the process would be decided locally.

Too impatient to let this process play out, though, the Standing Committee of the National People's Congress in Beijing, acting like a court, stepped in and handed down its verdict ahead of the local judges. Not only were Leung and Yau kept from taking office, but so were those who had performed much less overt acts of rebellion, including Law. In addition, when Agnes Chow attempted to run for the seat left open by Law's disqualification, she was stopped from doing so, on the grounds that Demosistō had promoted "independence" and thereby was not allowed to put forward a candidate. When Chow and her colleagues questioned this ruling, as the organization's stance had not changed since the time that Law was allowed to run, they were told that electoral officials needed to keep up with the times and shifts in legal interpretations.

In the end, the electoral results of 2016 proved a pyrrhic victory. The years following the emptying of the Occupy zones were overall a time of setbacks, when the heady sense of anything being possible that took hold during the Umbrella Movement dissipated. The political landscape increasingly seemed a deeply frustrating and sometimes impossible one to navigate.

Earlier this year, when my colleague Amy Hawkins interviewed Kong Tsung-gan, a veteran of the 2003 protests and participant in all the major upheavals since then, who wrote one of the first books about the Umbrella Movement, he referred to the period between 2015 and the start of 2019 as a time when a "deep depression" settled over many in Hong Kong. Young people were hit hard and were consumed by a "sense of failure" that he did not quite understand the roots of at first. In his eyes, the 2014 struggle had accomplished a lot, not in terms of concrete achievements but in providing people like himself with a feeling of empowerment and a knowledge that they were far from alone in caring about issues such as democracy. He gradually realized that there was a connection between the utopian highs of the movement's best moments and the despair that set in later, and that it was linked to generational differences. It was one thing, after all, "to know, intellectually, that the Communist Party is not going to give in right away. But it's another thing, especially when you are eighteen, nineteen, twenty years old," and have just gotten swept up in "the first big pro-democracy

66   thing you've participated in in your life, to be out there on the streets for seventy-nine days, and kind of give it your all, and come away with nothing."

I visited Hong Kong often during the period that Kong described as one when many people, especially young activists, felt disheartened. Each time I went there, I looked intently for signs of further erosion of Hong Kong's distinctiveness from mainland cities—and always found them. I also looked for signs that, even if Hong Kong was now a place where it could easily seem to activists as though a game was being played where the goalposts were being moved to make it hard for them to succeed, the territory remained very different from the cities just across the border on the mainland—and I always found those, too. Going there two or three times a year on average, I noticed on every visit more evidence of the language of the Communist Party seeping into Hong Kong via everything from government-sponsored propaganda to billboards for products and companies that played on Xi Jinping's favorite catchphrases, such as "Chinese Dream" (that was worked into a liquor ad on a bus) and "Belt and Road" (that was worked into an ad for a bank). Each time, though, I was cheered by seeing that at least one thing that I feared might have disappeared was still part of the local landscape.

It became a ritual for me during that period to visit the nearest university to take stock of what I could find that would be absent from a mainland campus. At the Chinese University of Hong Kong, for example, I would head to the base of the campus to look at the Goddess of Democracy, whose likeness is as taboo to portray in the mainland media as the Tank Man photo is. She was always right where she was supposed to be.

She did not, however, always look the same. One year I found
her draped with a black and white skirt. On the white stripes of
this garment, the names of more than a hundred jailed activists
were written. They were described on it as Hong Kong's first
"political prisoners." The list of names included that of Joshua
Wong, as well as dozens of youths about the same age or older
who were much less well known and usually serving consider-
ably longer sentences.

If I was nearer to the University of Hong Kong, I would go
to the area in front of the library where student groups put up
posters. When there, I would read with particular pleasure the
ones that strayed furthest into topical areas that could not be
discussed at Peking University in the capital or Fudan University
in Shanghai in the current tightly controlled era of Xi. I thought
particularly of the contrast with Fudan when I did this. This is
because in December 1986, when I was living on that campus,
its walls had been covered with proclamations of discontent, as
that was the time of a sort of warm-up for the Tiananmen protest wave that crested in Shanghai. By contrast, when I stayed at
the University of Hong Kong early in 1987, that campus seemed
a much less politically engaged institution than the one that I
had left behind in Shanghai. I do not remember seeing a single
political poster at the University of Hong Kong on that first
visit, in fact, and ended my first stay there convinced that edu-
cated youths on the mainland were much more interested in
protesting than their counterparts in the British colonial city.

If I was nearest to Hong Kong Baptist University when I
got to the city during the years following the Umbrella Movement, I headed to its Democracy Wall (*Minzhuqiang*). This term
is used for areas set aside for posters on several local campuses,

68   but I am particularly fond of the one at Baptist as it is easy to
      move from looking at the posters displayed there to gazing up
      at Lion Rock, a natural landmark that since 2014 has been firmly
      linked to democratic aspirations. The term *Minzhuqiang* is asso-
      ciated above all with a place in Beijing where protesters put
      up posters in 1978 and 1979 during what came to be called the
      Democracy Wall Movement. There was at least one Democ-
      racy Wall on a mainland campus as far back as the 1940s, when
      the ruling Nationalist Party was the organization activists were
      criticizing for stifling freedom of speech and thought. There
      was also a notable Democracy Wall at Peking University in the
      1950s, where students put up criticisms of the governing Com-
      munist Party during the "Hundred Flowers Campaign" in 1956,
      when Mao Zedong encouraged people to voice their true opin-
      ions of the regime, only to attack these critics a year later in the
      anti-rightist campaign of 1957–1959. My favorite memory of a
      trip to the Baptist University *Minzhuqiang* was when I saw it cov-
      ered with images of and quotes by Mao—reminding passersby
      that he had once said that those who suppress student move-
      ments will come to bad ends, and that he also, in a manner Hong
      Kong youths could relate to in the 2010s, had suggested that it
      might be best for his native Hunan Province to be able to break
      away from China, if being part of that country meant being con-
      trolled by dictatorial figures in Beijing. (In 2019, he reemerged
      in Hong Kong as protesters pasted one of his famous quotes on
      posters around the city: "A revolution is not a dinner party.")

          Seeing tangible reminders of Hong Kong's difference and
      freer public sphere was particularly welcome in those years,
      as each trip I took to the mainland left me despairing over how
      far Beijing had tightened the controls, a process that had begun

under Xi's predecessor, Hu Jintao. Taking part in events at both
the 2015 and 2016 Hong Kong International Literary Festival
that reflected on the Umbrella Movement felt significant, since
for decades the tendency on the mainland had been to squelch
all public discussion of recent protests. At a time when the web
across the mainland was being swept clean of images likening
the portly Xi Jinping to Winnie the Pooh, there was a frisson of
pleasure in working an image of the famous yellow bear wearing
a crown into the PowerPoint I used to accompany a Hong Kong
campus talk I gave in 2018. Memes on the mainland, quickly
censored, had used similar images to suggest that Xi saw himself as an emperor-like figure after altering the constitution to
allow his rule to continue until he chose to step down or died. It
was also reassuring to be able to buy books while in Hong Kong
that could not be sold on the mainland, even if it seemed to take
a little more effort to find them each time I went back to the city.
And when a trip to Hong Kong came right on the heels of a visit
to Shanghai or Beijing, it was a pleasure to get to a place where
Xi's face did not seem to be everywhere, staring out from the
cover of every magazine and television screen.

This said, it was hard to shake the sense that, since the end
of the Umbrella Movement, the differences between political
life in the territory and in other cities of the region were dimin-
ishing. It seemed possible that despair had taken such a toll that,
even if Hong Kong never became just like Shenzhen, it might
well become more like Macau, where taboo topics can be discussed but are often avoided; where there are some brave people
fighting to push back against increased mainland control, but
they often feel isolated. The dramatic new protest wave that
began in mid-2019 around the time of the thirtieth anniversary

of the June Fourth Massacre showed how far from dead the Lion Rock spirit of Hong Kong activism actually was; it showed that while post-Umbrella events were leading some to give up hope, they were making others ready to fight even harder for things they believed whenever a major new movement began. One of the things that studying the history of social movements has taught me is how hard it can be to tell if a struggle is over or whether it has merely entered a period of temporary dormancy. Even though the Umbrella Movement enjoyed global attention in 2014, it seemed that the world had stopped paying attention in the years thereafter, though Hong Kong was still in existential limbo—"liberty without democracy," as Chris Patten had put it. And now even those liberties were slowly disappearing.

I was in Hong Kong in November of 2018, when I had planned to attend the opening of the Badiucao art show, where Joshua Wong was scheduled to speak. I had met the activist twice before and looked forward to catching up with him. When the show was canceled, I figured I would not see him again until some future trip to Hong Kong. I was wrong, though, as he joined forces with two members of Pussy Riot who had also been scheduled to speak at the canceled event to hold a small protest against threats to free speech in the city. At the demonstration, Wong and the two Russian women arrived wearing balaclavas, the trademark garb of Pussy Riot. Wong pulled his off and began giving a talk, while the two members of Pussy Riot stood by holding up placards expressing support for Hong Kong's struggles and defending freedom of expression. After the short protest broke up, I saw Wong standing off to the side by himself. After I reintroduced myself and began reminding him of the fact that we had met a couple of times before, a smile spread across

his face and he said, in a tone of surprise edging toward wonder-
ment: "You remember me!"

I wondered at first whether he was intentionally being silly,
since he is someone I think about a lot. That did not seem likely,
though, as just before he noticed me walking toward him, he
had looked burned out and downcast. All of twenty-two years
old, Wong had already been fighting for Hong Kong's future
for more than a quarter of his life. Witnessing the slow death
of his hometown—not to mention being in prison—takes its
toll. Hong Kong was supposed to enjoy a variety of distinctive freedoms until 2047, among them universal suffrage. But
in reality Hong Kong was being altered by seemingly unstop-
pable processes—it was being squeezed. Its people had no vote,
and their voices were not heard, no matter how loudly they pro-
tested. Hong Kong is not just in its death throes, but is imag-
ined by some to have already died. Under these conditions, it is
no wonder that patriotic Hong Kongers have come to lose hope.
When your voice is not heard, you come to feel that you don't
matter—that you don't exist. I came to realize that Wong was
simply happy that *I remembered him*! He was genuinely heart-
ened by any sign that people outside of his city still cared.

Hong Kong as a place defined by liberties was disappearing,
but the fight for its identity and to preserve treasured aspects of
its civil society had gone largely unnoticed. It would take week
after week of massive street demonstrations, of wave after wave
of enormous civil discontent, to change that.

Battles

When the Occupy zones were finally abandoned late in 2014 — something that was widely interpreted as a success for the government's strategy of waging a war of attrition against the protesters and simply waiting them out — some protesters made final statements of defiance by writing on banners, posters, and blackboards a simple phrase: "We'll Be Back."

The Civil Human Rights Front is known for staging big protest events that are planned well in advance. These generally take place on symbolically charged dates, such as July 1. The organization also helps mount ad hoc demonstrations. One of these took place on April 28, 2019. Tens of thousands of people gathered that day to express their outrage at the sentencing of Benny Tai, Chan Kin-man, and other leaders of Occupy Central.

They also called for the withdrawal of a proposed extradition bill, which had not yet become globally famous and infamous. At present, Hong Kong has extradition treaties with twenty countries, but the new bill, introduced in February, would permit the Hong Kong government to entertain certain extradition requests from any nation—among them the PRC. Chief Executive Carrie Lam found a handy defense of the bill in the case of twenty-year-old Chan Tong-kai, a Hong Kong man who confessed to murdering his girlfriend in 2018 in Taiwan, a country with which Hong Kong has no extradition agreement. The new extradition bill, Lam said, would facilitate the return of Chan to Taiwan to face trial and allow justice to be done.

But the bill's many critics believed its real impetus lay not in Taiwan but in mainland China. That Hong Kong currently has no extradition agreement with the PRC speaks to the hallowed place the territory's judicial independence holds in the infrastructure of semi-autonomy guaranteed by the Basic Law. The new bill would change that, allowing Hong Kong to extradite people accused of certain crimes by the PRC across the border to the mainland. For many, the prospect called to mind the fate of the five abducted booksellers three years prior—people who had broken no Hong Kong laws, but faced draconian penalties under the nominally distinct mainland legal system. If passed, its critics said, the bill would amount to an unprecedented erasure of the political and legal autonomy Hong Kong had been promised.

Estimates of the crowd size for the April 28 protest ranged widely: The police said fewer than 30,000 people had marched, while the organizers claimed more than 120,000 had. No matter which estimate one believed, it was the biggest demonstration Hong Kong had seen since Lam became chief executive in 2017.

The Civil Human Rights Front was cheered by the turnout. Its members were convinced, though, that they could do better. Late in May, one of its leaders, Jimmy Sham, announced the group's plans for an ambitious follow-up march that would send a clear message to Lam to withdraw the hated bill, and would,

74   if successful, also show more generally that the post-Umbrella
       pattern of malaise interspersed with brief bursts of outrage was
       over, and that a time of sustained action was back. The date set
       for the march—for which the group sought and received official
       permission—was June 9. "If Carrie Lam isn't concerned about
       130,000 people," a May 21 article in the *Hong Kong Free Press*
       quoted Sham as saying, "this time we will aim for 300,000."

       More than three times that number of people turned
       out for the protest. On June 12, when the extradition bill was
       scheduled to be debated in the Legislative Council, protesters
       stormed the building amid tear gas and rubber bullets, stalling
       the legislative session. Lam and Police Commissioner Stephen
       Lo called the protest a "riot," sparking immediate outrage, espe-
       cially in the face of accusations of police brutality. The police
       later conceded that, of the thousands of protesters, only five
       "rioted." Three days later, Lam announced that the bill would
       be temporarily suspended—but refused to say it would be per-
       manently withdrawn. The next day, a giant march, which orga-
       nizers and police alike agreed was larger than the June 9 event
       and many think was the largest protest in Hong Kong's history,
       took place.

       Joshua Wong, who was sentenced to a jail term that was to
       last into July, was released on June 17. This was not completely
       unexpected, as prisoners jailed for minor offenses in Hong Kong
       are routinely released early if they behave well while incar-
       cerated; it seemed surprising, though, to observers used to
       tracking events in other parts of the People's Republic of China,
       in light of how much effort the authorities make in cities on the
       mainland to keep opposition figures controlled and unable to

participate in public activities. (In mid-August, Benny Tai was
set free on bail pending an appeal of his April conviction.)

As of October 2, 2019—the day I am finalizing this text—
the demonstrations have continued for well over three months
unabated. Protests have erupted every weekend—some large,
peaceful gatherings; others smaller, more spontaneous, and
often historically violent. Turnout at protests regularly numbers in the thousands. Even the larger, more sedate marches—
a longtime ritual by which Hong Kongers can express and cel-
ebrate their civil liberties—have erupted into violent clashes
with police at their fringes. The demonstrations have grown
somewhat smaller since the first flashpoints early in the
summer, but this is relative: Unlike during the Umbrella
Movement, where protests dwindled gradually and in many
respects of their own accord, momentum behind the 2019 protests remains strong.

Over the summer, the plan of attack on activists expanded to
include gatherings in settings not associated with demonstrations in the city's past, ranging from shopping malls to airport
arrival halls. More than a dozen Hong Kong Island, Kowloon,
and New Territory districts saw protests, acts of police repression, attacks on activists by thugs, or all of these things. For the
first time in local history protest rallies were held that were specifically designated as calls for action by mothers (who gathered in part to mock Carrie Lam's claim that she was a "mother"
to Hong Kong's people and viewed protesters as "spoiled children" needing to be disciplined), civil servants, health care
workers, and even elderly members of the community (who
referred to themselves as "gray hairs" who supported the youth

76   of the territory). There were not just new Lennon Walls put up
      at protest sites, in a repetition of what took place in 2014, but
      many variations on the Lennon Wall idea appeared—including
      "walking Lennon Walls," created when protesters covered their
      clothing and faces with Post-it notes.

      One key turning point came on July 21, when white-shirted
      thugs went on a rampage in the working-class neighborhood
      of Yuen Long, harming not just protesters but also passersby,
      while the police took no action against them. Other turning
      points came when, during the days immediately following
      the street fights, more protesters than gang members were
      arrested. Photographs and videos also began circulating online
      that showed police taking actions that looked just like those
      the thugs had taken.

      On August 5, the first general strike in Hong Kong's recent
      history took place. The city has had general strikes before, most
      notably in 1925, a time of intense anti-imperialist activity on
      the mainland that spread into Hong Kong. There were some dis-
      tinctively contemporary sides to this particular action, though,
      that made it very different from that early one. For example, as
      CNN reported, "more than 2,300 aviation workers joined the
      strike, according to the Hong Kong Federation of Trade Unions,
      leading to the cancellation of 224 flights to and from one of
      the world's busiest airports." It also stood out from previous
      post-1997 protests, which tended to be localized. On August
      5, according to CNN again, protest actions "took place in seven
      districts" spread across the territory—and even Hong Kong
      Disneyland on isolated Lantau Island was affected. Neither the
      Umbrella Movement nor the 1989 protest wave had crossed
      lines of class and geography so forcefully and quickly, leading

experts to either bring up 1925 or the special case of 1967 as the
only events of comparable scope.

While the protesters defied recent precedents with the
strike, the authorities began breaking recent precedent in a different way: routinely turning down requests to hold marches in
standard locales, requests of a type that during the first decades
after the Handover were routinely approved. In the middle of
August, just as there were calls in many quarters for protesters
to make a renewed commitment to nonviolent rallies, the government rejected a Civil Human Rights Front application to hold
a daylong march, on a Sunday, along a standard route. All they
would allow was a one-hour rally. The government became even
more restrictive in giving permission for assemblies during the
following weeks.

It was also clear, especially by the final weeks of the summer
and first weeks of the fall, when frustration with the limited
results of nonviolent actions led a small percentage of activists
to begin lobbing Molotov cocktails and setting fires on streets
and at MTR entrances, that the level of violence by protesters,
while mainly causing harm to property and only in isolated
incidents to people, would far exceed that seen in 2014. On the
side of the opponents of the movement, it became clear early
on that the authorities were much less reticent than five years
before about using harsher measures, with police even firing
live rounds of ammunition on October 1 (something they had
not done earlier in 2019 or in 2014); on a day when clashes in the
city competed with the lavish National Day parade in Beijing for
global media attention, a police officer shooting a youth in the
chest at close range became a major news story. It also became
clear early on that the chief executive would be less visible

78 and make fewer public comments. Lam virtually disappeared from view for weeks soon after her off-key comment about acting as a "mother" to the city. There were also more ginned-up pro-police rallies and parades designed to show support for the CCP and the local authorities, sometimes involving groups who came over from the mainland to participate, than there had been in earlier years. (This is not to suggest that Hong Kong lacks residents who simply oppose the protests and do not need prodding to join these events. It has them. There are some recent migrants from across the border, for example, who feel people with longer histories in the territory look down on them as less cultured. There are people who supported the protests early on but then were dismayed by acts of vandalism that, while rare, were magnified in the coverage of the events that some locals depend on. And so on.)

The movement, which had very broad if by no means universal support among Hong Kong's residents, had six objectives. First, it called for the permanent and formal withdrawal of the extradition bill. Second, arrested protesters and political prisoners were to be released. Third, an independent commission would be set up to investigate police brutality over the course of many of the protests, but particularly during the clashes of June 12. Fourth, the SAR government was to retract its characterization of the protests as "riots." The fifth demand called for Lam to resign, and the sixth stipulation was for universal suffrage to be immediately implemented, with the Legislative Council and the chief executive being directly elected. (Often, the call is for "five demands" to be met, not one less, with the resignation of Lam left off; sometimes, early in the fall, protesters added a new demand: the disbanding of the police force.)

On July 9, Lam called the bill "dead" but refused to withdraw it. On September 4, Lam finally announced that the bill would be formally withdrawn. With only one of six objectives met, the protests and civil disobedience raged on.

The most surprising aspect of the movement is simply how long it has lasted. Why continue to protest, when it seems so incredibly unlikely that the authorities would be willing to budge on the issues that have become most central to the struggle? There is no easy answer to this question that is being asked now almost as often as the "will there be a replay of the June Fourth Massacre" was during much of the summer. The not strictly accurate notion that frogs will allow themselves to be boiled alive, provided that a pot's temperature is turned up slowly, can help us understand the phenomenon. The idea was employed effectively recently by Canny Leung in an editorial in the *Apple Daily*, the most daring of Hong Kong's major Chinese-language periodicals. "The Frogs of Hong Kong have all been in one big pot and the water temperature has gradually been rising. Early on, some Frogs jumped out of the pot; others have struggled to cope with the increasing heat; and then there are those Frogs who have gone mad in their death throes," Leung wrote. "We've all been in that pot of hot water for twenty-two years. Now and then, they suddenly turn up the heat to see how the Frogs will react. If we don't struggle too violently they know they can apply more heat next time around. That's why it's been getting hotter and hotter and the heat has been turned up with ever greater frequency."

The extradition law was yet another click upward of the flame, but one that was even more noticeable than some of the others. People are protesting and continuing to protest— because they feel that the pot is close to the final boiling point.

80   One activist recently interviewed in the *New Yorker* referred to a doomsday clock reaching its final minute in Hong Kong. Countdown clocks have long figured in the Hong Kong story. Before 1997, the CCP put a large one up in Tiananmen Square, ticking off the seconds until the colony returned, in official parlance, to the embrace of the ancestral homeland. From the time of the Handover, Hong Kong has been promised a fifty-year grace period until full integration, with 2047 now the endpoint. A doomsday clock takes that idea and gives it a dramatic dark twist. The idea now is that Hong Kong as it has been will disappear well before 2047. Protesters can dream about reversing the trend, but all they can realistically expect to be able to do is throw themselves onto the gears of the machine to slow its progress.

A song that can help us understand the continuity of the struggle is "Do You Hear the People Sing?" As the poet, translator, and editor Tammy Ho noted in the immediate aftermath of the Umbrella Movement, there is an interesting difference between the lyrics to the English and Cantonese versions of the song, both of which were sung on the streets of Hong Kong in 2014 and have been sung there again this year. In the Cantonese version, the idea becomes not a query directed upwards asking those in power if they are listening but instead imploring the populace to show their mettle. In the Hong Kong version, the opening question is: "Who has not spoken out yet?" Different social groups feel the need to prove their devotion to a beloved community by marching or rallying, and the movement has been carried forward in part by events geared toward specific groups, with different sectors of society joining stalwarts of the movement and various moments in marches and rallies specifically geared toward, at various moments, senior citizens, financial workers, mothers, and so on. While the government hoped that the movement would peter out when the new academic year began in September, this was not the case at all. By contrast, it was reinvigorated by middle school students joining those who had been protesting for months.

Another song, "Glory to Hong Kong," was written midway through the current movement, and gradually took on a dual role as an anthem of the struggle and a song for the city—a counterpart to the Chinese national anthem. One thing that can end a movement is ennui and boredom. New tactics—including forming the "Hong Kong Way," a human chain thirty miles long, inspired by and staged on the thirtieth anniversary of the "Baltic Way," when two million people formed a human chain spanning more than four hundred miles across Estonia, Latvia, and Lithuania in support of independence from the Soviet Union—helped refresh and reenergize protesters, but so did this novel song, which was suddenly, it seemed, being performed everywhere (from schoolyards to malls) and by all kinds of ensembles (including, in one popular video, a philharmonic group clothed in black and wearing gas masks). The SAR government's leaders had made it clear in 2018 that they believed a mainland law making it illegal to show disrespect for the PRC's national anthem, which carried a sentence of up to three years in prison, should be applied in Hong Kong. An alternative national anthem illustrates just how much Hong Kong independence has grown from a fringe idea prior to 2019 to a more mainstream one. On September 10, before a World Cup qualifying football match, protesters booed the Chinese national anthem, and broke into a rendition of "Glory to Hong Kong."

The current crisis hitting Hong Kong is unique. History does not repeat itself—and one reason is that both protesters and the authorities are influenced by past occurrences they have lived through or learned about. Their interest in avoiding replicating past outcomes alters equations, and the other variables involved are never quite the same as during a previous crisis. There are, however, always imperfect but useful analogies that can help place a new crisis into perspective. Some posters referred to the August 5 general strike as a "triple stoppage" (*sanba* in Mandarin), meaning that students stopped going to classes, workers stopped working, and merchants stopping selling. The first important "triple stoppages" took place in Shanghai in 1919 and 1925 to protest both imperialist actions and police brutality against protesters, and the first important Hong Kong general strike, partly inspired by the second Shanghai one, took place in the latter year. In the 1940s, when Shanghai was controlled by the Nationalist Party, the authorities mobilized thugs to attack protesters, claimed that large demonstrations supported by the Communist Party were solely the work of foreign agents and did not reflect true popular sentiment, and ginned up pro-stability "protests"—all tactics that supporters of the Communist Party have used in recent weeks in Hong Kong.

In 1950, the newly founded People's Republic invaded Tibet, and the Communist Party imposed a Seventeen Point Agreement on the area. The declaration promised Tibetans that they would be able to enjoy a high degree of autonomy, but nine years later a full-scale occupation put an end to this "One Country, Two Systems" *avant la lettre* arrangement. If People's Liberation Army troops move into Hong Kong the way they moved into

Tibet six decades before, 2019 could be seen by historians of the future as having a valence for Hong Kongers that 1959 has for Tibetans. In traditional Chinese numerology, sixty-year cycles have a significance similar to what centuries have traditionally had in the West.

Carrie Lam's position in the current crisis is comparable in some ways to that of leaders of East Germany and neighboring states decades ago when they were confronted with popular protests. She claims to represent the people of Hong Kong, just as leaders of East Germany and Poland, for example, claimed to represent the people of those lands, but her actions have been shaped, as those proxies to Moscow were then, by signals sent from a capital hundreds of miles away. One reason there was no crackdown on protests in Leipzig and East Berlin thirty years ago was that Mikhail Gorbachev had made it clear that he was not in favor of East German leaders employing what was sometimes then called a "Chinese Solution" to the problem— meaning, in the wake of the June Fourth Massacre, using deadly force. The result was an end to Communist Party rule in East Germany during a year that also saw dramatic changes in many neighboring countries. This kind of result has never been in the cards for the Hong Kong crisis, as Xi Jinping, like his immediate predecessors, views Gorbachev as someone who took the wrong course of action.

Overall, Hong Kong is in a far more chaotic and fraught state than it was at any point during the Umbrella Movement. Indeed, things are more on edge than they have been at any moment since the Handover. What the current movement has achieved is to put Beijing on notice, to show that if Hong Kong's autonomy is wilting so, too, is the grand experiment of "One

84   Country, Two Systems" dying. Much depends on how China
       handles the civil disobedience as it stands in the global spot-
       light. But China has grown into a superpower far stronger than
       it had been in 1959 or 1989, and increasingly cares little about
       what Thatcher's "forum of the world" thinks of its actions. Will
       China ever genuinely keep its promise of implementing actual
       democracy in Hong Kong? Can Hong Kong's discontent con-
       vince China to give in to calls for universal suffrage? I don't
       think that's even the question to ask anymore. Rather, will the
       resistance be able to stop the erosion of Hong Kong's hopes and
       liberties? Years of Beijing moving the goalposts make it seem
       unlikely. What is clear is that "liberty without democracy"
       has torn Hong Kong apart, and that this Special Administra-
       tive Region cannot survive in its current state. China might not
       occupy the territory as it did in Tibet, or send in tanks as it did
       in Beijing. It's become clear, however, that there is little stop-
       ping Beijing from destroying many of Hong Kong's institutions,
       even if it continues to be frustrated, as other colonizers in Ire-
       land and many other places were in the past, in its inability to
       stamp out attachment to signs of local identity and crush the
       Lion Rock spirit.

Water

Hong Kong has long been a place with varied and deep associations with water. "Harbor" is the second term in its two-character name, coming after a word most often translated as "fragrant." Fish and seafood figure centrally in the storied local cuisine. Hong Kong first gained economic importance due to its role as a hub of trade involving vessels that moved goods across rivers and seas. Humid air, mist, and the torrents of water that lash the city during typhoons are key parts of the local climate. Umbrellas served as protest symbols in 2014. While the city teetered on the brink in 2019, activists, striving to create a new alternative world in the streets and in malls and in airport arrival and departure halls in the midst of scenes of destruction, urged one another to "be water," to adapt their tactics continually to changing circumstances. To resemble "water" means to be flexible in one's actions, going one place but quickly heading to another if there is too much resistance. The idea can be traced back to long-standing Chinese philosophical traditions, especially Daoism (though metaphors linked to water are important in Confucian texts as well). It has a more specific referent, though, to perhaps the most famous Hong Konger, martial artist and movie star Bruce Lee. "Don't get set into one form, adapt it and build your own, and let it grow. Be like water," he said. "Empty your mind, be formless, shapeless—like water. Now you put water in a cup, it becomes the cup. You put water into a bottle it becomes the bottle. You put it in a teapot it becomes the teapot. Now water can flow, or it can crash! Be water, my friend."

The air was filled with pepper spray and tear gas that looked from the distance like fog, and young men and young women moved to douse canisters of the latter noxious substance with water. Police late in the summer began to turn water cannons on crowds, using liquid dyed blue so that they would be able to tell later who to arrest. It is fitting, then, that images linked to water—from an activist's comment that Hong Kong's fate is like that of the ship in a famous film with a tragic ending, to Lord Patten's reference to the speed of snow melting, to Leung's commentary about Hong Kongers being like frogs in a pot whose temperature keeps coming closer to a deadly boil—have appeared throughout the preceding pages.

There's also the metaphor of the hundred-year flood, the (inaccurate) myth that rivers overflow their banks once a century. Just as the 2019 protest movement was underway in Hong Kong, the author Adam Hochschild published a powerful essay about the parallels of American politics in the years 1919 and 2019. Hochschild conjured up the image of a very particular sort of hundred-year flood: the unleashing of ugly nativist rhetoric in America during the presidency of Woodrow Wilson, and now again during that of Donald Trump. With events treated in the preceding chapters on my mind, his essay set me wondering whether there were parallels and imperfect analogies linked to events of a century ago worth considering when trying to make sense of the current Hong Kong crisis. There are, I think—providing that once again we place Shanghai's past beside Hong Kong's present.

What exactly happened in the great port city of the Yangzi Delta one hundred years ago? There was a dramatic series of protests in which young people took leading roles. There was a general strike, Shanghai's first triple stoppage. On the whole, the protesters behaved in peaceful ways, but there were some ugly incidents, during which they roughed up people they viewed as outsiders. One goal of the movement was to stop a widely disliked document from going into effect. The protesters directed much of their ire at government officials they viewed as immoral and too ready to do the bidding of men in a distant capital. They also called for the release of protesters who had been arrested and complained about police using too much force in dealing with demonstrators. The movement became in large part a fight for the right to speak out. The protests in the city were preceded by, built on, and expanded a repertoire of action developed during a series of earlier struggles, as some participants in the 1919 demonstrations had been part of shorter waves of activism in 1915 and 1918 and in some cases even in 1905. New tactics were added to the mix in 1919. So were new symbols: For example, a distinctive type of headwear became associated with the protests, as students eschewed wearing straw hats made in Japan for locally made cotton ones.

This analogy is far from perfect. The Shanghai protests of 1919 were part of a nationwide struggle, known as the May Fourth Movement, in honor of the day of the year's first major demonstration, which took place in Beijing. The current crisis, by contrast, began and has stayed centered in Hong Kong, as did the Umbrella Movement before it. The biggest mass gatherings in Shanghai in 1919 did not involve more than a few thousand people, while the largest in Hong Kong in 2019 have been exponentially bigger in size. There have been many more arrests this year, and there were no paving stones thrown or fires set by activists in Shanghai a century ago. The document the protesters of 1919 disliked was not a local bill but an international accord: The Treaty of Versailles, the post–World War I agreement that they objected to because it passed control of former German possessions in Shandong Province to Japan rather than returning them to Chinese control. While one student died from the injuries he received at the hands of the police during the initial protest on May 4, 1919, many fewer demonstrators and bystanders were injured in any part of China one hundred years ago than have been injured in Hong Kong during 2019. While cotton hats were preferred to straw ones in 1919 because the latter were made in Japan, the importance of hard hats in this year's crisis has had pragmatic as well as symbolic significance.

The protesters of 1919 even succeeded in gaining more concessions from the warlords in control of Beijing than those of 2019 have managed to secure. In the immediate wake of the Shanghai General Strike, which stands out as one of the most important of all May Fourth Movement collective actions, three officials that the students claimed were too cozy with Tokyo were removed from their positions and the protesters arrested in Beijing were released. The Chinese delegation to the Paris Peace Conference, who had a role in the proceedings as both China and Japan had come into World War I on the side of the Allies, refused to sign the Treaty of Versailles. These successes by the protesters help to explain why the May Fourth Movement has long been hailed in China as a triumphant struggle. By contrast, while Carrie Lam withdrew the extradition law in September, there have been no moves toward concession regarding the other key demands of the Hong Kong protesters. The authorities have not released those who have been arrested, appointed an independent commission to investigate allegations of police violence, or retracted their description of early protests as "riots." Lam has not resigned, and there is no universal suffrage in Hong Kong.

But while the May Fourth Movement has a hallowed place in Chinese history now, it was for decades considered largely a failure. While the Chinese delegation to Paris refused to sign the Treaty of Versailles, the accord went into effect anyway. Former German territories in Shandong fell under Japanese control. The May Fourth activists failed to prevent territory they cared about from going from the control of one colonial power to another. And the Japanese seizure of Shandong, which was preceded by its seizing of Korea and Taiwan, was followed in 1931 by Tokyo taking Manchuria and later moving further into China and other neighboring lands.

Japan asserted in many cases that it was not taking over territories, but freeing them from colonial rule, and allowing them to be governed at last by locals. They made this claim about Shanghai, proclaiming in the early 1940s that it was finally liberated from all forms of foreign control, even as Japanese troops and Chinese puppet officials controlled the city. They made this claim about Manchuria as they put Pu Yi, the ethnically Manchu former Last Emperor of the Qing Dynasty, on the throne, as a ruler beholden to Tokyo. They did not talk of

90   a single empire with multiple systems, but rather of a Greater East Asian Co-Prosperity Sphere. Beijing, too, does not talk of having an empire, but its handling of Tibet and Xinjiang rhymes with Tokyo's imperial approach. Beijing's dreams for Hong Kong, which are nightmares to those on the streets, rhyme with Tokyo's proclamations about Shanghai. The terms are new— "One Country, Two Systems," "Greater Bay Area"—but when it comes to fantasies and raw power, there are disturbing echoes.

History does not repeat itself. And yet, this is a time when some in Hong Kong wonder if their city's fate will parallel that of Tibet decades ago. Some in Taipei remember well that when the "One Country, Two Systems" framework was first proposed, the Communist Party suggested that someday Taiwan, too, could become a Special Administrative Region of the People's Republic.

History does not repeat itself. In 1919, the Western powers actively aided Japan's move into Shandong. Viewed within a hundred-year framework, the limited international concern about Hong Kong's fate is deeply worrying. So, too, are the signals some world leaders, including Vladimir Putin and Donald J. Trump, have been sending to Xi Jinping during the current crisis, which convey a sense that whatever he does will be just fine with them, as long as it does not impinge on their plans for their own nations. Hundred-year floods can wreak many different kinds of damage.

History does not repeat itself. Even the most attractive analogies need to be used with care. Between the time that this book goes into production in October 2019 and the time it appears early in 2020, many things may become clearer. However, 2019 will clearly go down in history as a year that, like 1919, marks an important turning point in the history of protest, repression, and imperial projects in East Asia.

This short book was written quickly. In spite but in some ways because of this, in completing it I have accumulated a long list of debts of gratitude. I needed to draw on the expertise, insights and experiences of a lot of individuals, many based in Hong Kong, to try to keep up with a rapidly unfolding story and still meet tight deadlines. Many busy people graciously made time to talk to me about the project (either in formal interview settings or more often informally), offer advice, or read drafts— and in some cases do all of those things. I was touched by how many said they were happy to make the time because they felt that helping me get this book into the world was a small way of giving back to a city they loved. I could not have completed the book without their help.

In addition, I could not have done what I have without the extraordinary support I got from all the members of the special Columbia Global Reports team. For example, Nicholas Lemann provided early guidance on framing the book that was key, while Jimmy So did so much to improve the drafts of chapters that I sent him that I felt at times we were coauthoring a volume.

Four other people deserve heartfelt thanks at the outset. Three of them are Nash Jenkins, Hana Meihan Davis, and Chit Wai John Mok. Each has deep affection for and a keen understanding of Hong Kong, and each carved out large chunks of time to help when I had major deadlines drawing near. Each aided me in sharpening my thinking on key issues and avoiding mistakes, and Nash also kept me on track to finish the work on time by

92   chasing down references and not only polishing paragraphs but crafting more than a few sentences from scratch. I owe him a lot, but I owe even more to Amy Hawkins: for research support, archival digging, interviewing, and other assistance that she provided throughout this project. It is a much better book than it could have been without working with her on it. I feel very fortunate to have been able to benefit from the talents of all four of these talented young writers.

Advice I got early in the writing process from Emilie Tran saved me from going astray, and I also need to thank her for hosting a memorable dinner party in Hong Kong at which conversations that shaped central arguments took place. I received valuable comments on specific sections and specific ideas from Yvonne Yu, Elaine Yu, John Carroll, Ian Johnson, Didi Kirsten Tatlow, Gina Tam, James Carter, Edmund Cheng, Lev Nachman, Denise Y. Ho (the historian), Lauren Hilgers, and Isabel Hilton. In a category all their own, James Griffiths and Sebastian Veg went beyond the call of duty—and indeed of friendship—in providing close readings of and comments on the entire work. My understanding of Hong Kong has been enriched by years of conversations with Zoher Abdoolcarim, Ilaria Maria Sala, Louisa Lim, Jeffrey Ngo, Liam Fitzgerald, David Bandurski, and Suzanne Sataline, as well as many of the people already mentioned above. I have learned key things about the city through intensive exchanges during recent months with Geremie Barmé and Debbie Davis—both people I already owed for the help they had given me on totally different topics in the past.

I also have people I need to thank for quite specific reasons—
from steering me to sources, to sharing key experiences in Hong
Kong, to encouraging or discouraging me from pursuing partic-
ular analogies, to carving out time to answer my questions, to
editing or cowriting short pieces that were reworked into sections of this book. Those in this capacious category include the
following: Ian Rowen, Chris Buckley, Mike Forsythe, Jason Y.
Ng, Suzanne Pepper, Chris Patten, Timothy Garton Ash, Hsiung
Ping-Chen, Poo Mu-Chou, Rana Mitter, Antony Dapiran,
Christine Loh, Austin Ramzy, Anthony Kuhn, Florence de
Changy, Nick Serpe, Michael Kazin, Robert Bickers, Paul Cohen,
John Gittings, Mishi Saran, Elizabeth Sinn, Joe Piscatella, Phil-
lipa Milne, Anya Goncharova, Kellee Tsai, David Zweig, Ste-
phen Platt, Eric Florence, Benjamin Haas, Brian Spivey, Gavin
Jacobson, Ben Bland, Victor Mallet, Tammy Ho Lai-Ming, Eric
Sautedé, Prashant Rao, Tom Lutz, Stéphanie Giry, Ma Ngok,
Andrea Lingenfelter, Samson Yuen, Angelina Chin, Tim Oakes,
Yidi Wu, Margot Landman, Maura Cunningham, Jeffrey Kop-
stein, Xue Yiwei, Alan Wong, Amy Wilentz and Ching Kwan Lee.
Needless to say, no one thanked above should be held responsible for any of the opinions expressed in this book, nor, of
course, any of the errors it contains.

Finally, I want to express my gratitude to two people who I spent
time with in 1987 during my first weeks in Hong Kong. One is
Anne Bock. I've thanked her before but am doing so here for
helping me make sense of and appreciate a city that back then
was new to both of us; putting up (not for the first time) with
my becoming so obsessed with a topic that for a time it seemed
all that I was able to talk and think about; and (again, not for

94   the first time) listening to and commenting on my stories about
that topic, and in the process helping me decide which I should
and which I shouldn't try to put on the page.

Last but not least, I want to express thanks to someone who,
alas, did not live long enough to read these acknowledgments
or indeed any part of this book about the city he loved: Ming
K. Chan. This historian of the Pearl River Delta died just before
I began working on *Vigil*. He was my first guide to Hong Kong,
equally adept at introducing me to its history and to its food.
He was the first person to invite me to present my work at a
local university. He also was prescient enough to tell me in 2013
that I would never forgive myself if I ended a short stay in Hong
Kong without making time to go with him to meet and talk to a
teenager he had gotten to know who he described, in a typically
for him over-the-top manner, as a one-of-a-kind "super kid!"
The teenager in question was Joshua Wong. Ming was right
that I would have always regretted failing to meet that unusual
youth. I remember thinking then that Wong would probably
never be more famous than he was at that point, when he was
well known in Hong Kong for his role in the 2012 protest wave
but far from a household name anywhere else. I was completely
wrong, of course. That was neither the first nor the last time
I made an erroneous prediction relating to Hong Kong, a city
that has long been, and I hope will somehow long continue to
be, a place of surprises.

CHAPTER ONE

Ackbar Abbas, *Hong Kong: Culture and the Politics of Disappearance*. Minneapolis: University of Minnesota Press, 1997
A prescient meditation, which was published months before the 1997 Handover, that reflects on how Hong Kong has grappled with its cultural identity in its precarious geographical, cultural, and political setting.

John M. Carroll, *A Concise History of Hong Kong*. Lanham, Maryland: Rowman and Littlefield, 2007
An authoritative historical survey of colonial Hong Kong, beginning with the years ahead of British colonization and concluding with the aftermath of the 1997 Handover.

Chan Ho-Kei, *The Borrowed*, translated by Jeremy Tiang. New York: Black Cat, 2017
A novel, or more correctly a collection of six novellas, following a detective on the Hong Kong police force through the territory's political upheavals across the end of the 1900s and the beginning of the twenty-first century.

Antony Dapiran, *City of Protest: A Recent History of Dissent in Hong Kong*. Sydney: Penguin Specials, 2017
A brief but definitive account of the many moments of political turmoil that have floored Hong Kong since the leftist riots of the late 1960s, urging us to understand the city's unique political identity through its tradition of civil disobedience. One of several works in Penguin's compelling series offering varied perspectives on contemporary Hong Kong.

Dung Kai-cheung, *Atlas: The Archaeology of an Imaginary City*. New York: Columbia University Press, 2012
The City of Victoria is Dung's gentle fictionalization of Hong Kong, depicted from the perspective of future archaeologists who are studying a metropolis that has since vanished. "Victoria" is similar to its real-world counterpart not just physically but spiritually: The book is Dung's attempt to grapple with the political anxieties of Hong Kong at the cusp of the millennium and anticipate their dark conclusion.

96 **Tammy Ho Lai-Ming, Jason Y. Ng, and Mishi Saran, editors,**
    Hong Kong 20/20: Reflections on a Borrowed Place. **Hong Kong:**
    Blacksmith Books, 2017
    Here, PEN Hong Kong—an organization dedicated to free speech issues—
    assembles some of the most prominent and eloquent Hong Kong voices
    to offer a stark reflection on the city's political and cultural anxieties in
    the years since the Handover. Includes, along with pieces by the editors,
    contributions by Joshua Wong, Ilaria Maria Sala, and Louisa Lim.

Lai-Chu Hon, *The Kite Family,* **translated by Andrea Lingenfelter.**
Hong Kong: Hong Kong University Press, 2015
Lai-Chu Hon is perhaps Hong Kong's most imaginative literary writer
today. This collection of short stories, translated from Cantonese, tracks a
series of darkly surreal and yet unnervingly real characters. The tales paint
a picture of a culture both dystopian and mundane.

Brian Ladd, *The Ghosts of Berlin: Confronting German History in the*
Urban Landscape. **Chicago: University of Chicago Press, 1997**
How does the aesthetic of a place transmit the ghosts of its history? Ladd
carries this question through Germany's most cosmopolitan city, finding in
its architecture and culture the shadows of a tumultuous history.

John le Carré, *The Honourable Schoolboy.* **New York: Knopf, 1977**
Le Carré's novel both showcases his strengths as a weaver of intrigue and
offers a gripping portrait of British Hong Kong in the throes of the Cold
War. Those acquainted with Hong Kong will encounter some familiar
settings, most famously the bar of the Foreign Correspondents' Club.

Jan Morris, *Hong Kong.* **New York: Random House, 1988**
This acclaimed travel writer's love letter to Hong Kong remains one of
the sharpest and most enjoyable portraits of the city. That this is still true
despite the city's political and cultural evolution in the three decades since
Hong Kong's first publication is a testament to how well the author captures
the soul of the place.

FILMS

In the Mood for Love, **directed by Wong Kar-wai, 2000**
Wong is arguably the best-known auteur to emerge from Hong Kong's
legendary film industry, and this film reminds us why. It follows two lovers
across their affair in 1960s-era Hong Kong, exploring the lives of those
Shanghainese refugees who tenuously built lives for themselves in the
territory after the Chinese revolution.

***The Pacific Century—The Two Coasts of China*, produced by Alex Gibney, 1992**
This documentary was written as well as produced by Alex Gibney, who is best known for his more recent work on political and cultural scandals and the people who inhabit them: The Church of Scientology, former New York governor Eliot Spitzer, Theranos' Elizabeth Holmes. In this earlier project (a segment in an extended series), he offers insights into China's changing place in the world and its ambivalent imperial aspirations.

***Ten Years*, an anthology film directed by Jevons Au, Kiwi Chow, Zune Kwok, Ka-Leung Ng, and Fei-Pang Wong, 2015**
Perhaps the most talked-about Hong Kong film made in the aftermath of the 2014 Umbrella Movement, *Ten Years* anticipates a city a decade in the future: one where mainland Chinese encroachment has run its course. For many Hong Kongers, its pessimistic prophecy was less speculative than already present.

CHAPTER TWO

Ming K. Chan, editor, *China's Hong Kong Transformed: Retrospect and Prospects Beyond the First Decade*. Hong Kong: City University of Hong Kong Press, 2008
A collection of clear-eyed takes on of the first decade of Hong Kong after the Handover and its future ahead of 2047, when the tenuous contract of "one country, two systems" expires. The editor began as a specialist in the history of labor activism in various parts of the Pearl River Delta, but in his final years focused increasingly on current events in his native Hong Kong and helping to build the field of Hong Kong studies.

Stephen Chiu, Tai-Lok Lui, *Hong Kong: Becoming a Chinese Global City*. London: Routledge, 2009
A useful study of what China's economic flourishing has meant for the city that was for years —but is no longer—its greatest financial and commercial powerhouse.

Danny Gittings, *Introduction to The Hong Kong Basic Law*, 2nd edition. Hong Kong: University of Hong Kong, 2018
The authoritative analysis of Hong Kong's dense, complicated constitution, useful to legal experts and curious students alike.

Syd Goldsmith, *Hong Kong on the Brink: An American Diplomat Relives 1967's Darkest Days*. Hong Kong: Blacksmith Books, 2017
In the late 1960s, Goldsmith was the only white diplomat in Hong Kong's

98   American Consulate who spoke Cantonese; here, half a century later, he
      recounts his experience of the violent riots and upheavals that upended the
      city at the end of that decade.

Chris Patten, *East and West*. New York: MacMillan, 1999
Here, the last colonial governor of Hong Kong recounts his political
leadership of the city in the years preceding the transition to Chinese
rule and the uncertain future beyond it. Patten speaks at length about
his efforts to safeguard the territory's civil liberties, and the hostility it
provoked in Beijing.

**Steve Tsang, *A Modern History of Hong Kong: 1841–1997*. London:
I.B. Tauris, 2003**
Another comprehensive history of the territory from the colonization of
the "barren rock" to the 1997 transfer of sovereignty to China.

**Stephen Vines, *Hong Kong: China's New Colony*. London: Aurum
Press, 1998**
The veteran journalist Vines, among the best-known English-language
commentators in contemporary Hong Kong, offers a no-holds-barred look
at what Chinese rule has meant for the world's freest city.

**Eilo W. Y. Yu and Ming K. Chan, editors, *China's Macao Transformed:
Challenge and Development in the 21st Century*. Hong Kong: City
University of Hong Kong Press, 2014**
A necessary look at the lesser-known Special Administrative Region across
the Pearl River Delta from Hong Kong. The book takes particular interest
in Macau's political struggles and democratic shortcomings in the decades
since the end of Portuguese rule.

FILMS

***The Gate of Heavenly Peace*, directed by Carma Hinton and Richard
Gordon, 1995**
A gripping three-hour account of the mainland Chinese protests in 1989
and the June 4 Massacre. The documentary offers useful and eloquent
context for the viewer unfamiliar with contemporary China.

***Made in Hong Kong*, directed by Fruit Chan, 1997**
A drama that introduced many international viewers to the dizzying
claustrophobia of life in Hong Kong's public housing skyscrapers,
capturing the ennui and anxieties of the city ahead of the 1997 Handover.

CHAPTER THREE

Ben Bland, *Generation HK: Seeking Identity in China's Shadow.* Sydney: Penguin Specials, 2017

A short and compelling look at the young generation born on the cusp of the Handover and the political revolution they have mobilized. Bland has a valuable chapter on protesters of Agnes Chow and Joshua Wong's generation, but also takes up less expected subjects, such as the views and lifestyles of the children of tycoons.

Ming-sho Ho, *Challenging Beijing's Mandate of Heaven: Taiwan's Sunflower Movement and Hong Kong's Umbrella Movement.* Philadelphia: Temple University Press, 2019

Ho aligns two coeval political flashpoints in two places commonly regarded as both Chinese and not: the Umbrella protests in Hong Kong and the Sunflower Movement in Taiwan, which called for the country's government to withdraw its free-trade agreement with Hong Kong. A portrait of the anxieties that have flourished through life in China's orbit.

Kong Tsung-gan, *Umbrella: A Political Tale from Hong Kong.* Hong Kong: Pema Press, 2017

A well-known online commentator in Hong Kong, Kong combines memoir and analysis in this account of three months of protest at the end of 2014. His personal perspective enriches the historical and political context in which he situates events.

Ching Kwan Lee and Ming Sing, editors, *Take Back Our Future: An Eventful History of the Hong Kong Umbrella Movement.* Ithaca: Cornell University Press, 2019

This recent work lends the scope of political theory to the 2014 unrest in Hong Kong, offering a refreshing and vital perspective transcending the familiar political and historical narrative. The introduction by Lee, who did acclaimed work on topics such as labor activism on the Chinese mainland and China's role in Africa before shifting to focusing most on her native Hong Kong, is superb.

Francis L.F. Lee and Joseph M. Chan, *Media and Protest Logics in the Digital Era: The Umbrella Movement in Hong Kong.* Oxford: Oxford University Press, 2018

A crucial study of the vital role media and communications technologies played in both Hong Kong's 2014 protests and the political discontent that motivated them. The authors have continued to track the issues they address in the book through the current crisis.

100 **Ngok Ma and Edmund Cheng editors,** *The Umbrella Movement:*
Civil Resistance and Contentious Space in Hong Kong. **Amsterdam:**
University of Amsterdam Press, 2019
This collection examines the currents and practices of civil disobedience
that coalesced in the form of the Umbrella Movement, and what it might
mean to challenge a hegemonic power in the world's densest city. Among
its strongest chapters is one by Sebastian Veg.

Jason Y. Ng, *Umbrellas in Bloom: Hong Kong's Occupy Movement*
Uncovered. **Hong Kong: Blacksmith Books, 2016**
A celebratory remembrance of the 2014 demonstrations, buoyed by Ng's
intelligent insights into Hong Kong's cultural fabric and access to some of
the Umbrella Movement's most vital players.

Suzanne Pepper, *Keeping Democracy at Bay: Hong Kong and the*
Challenge of Chinese Political Reform. **Lanham, Maryland: Rowman**
and Littlefield, 2007
Pepper, an astute and insightful commentator on and longtime resident in
Hong Kong, lends her expertise to understanding the legacy of the city's
colonial infrastructure, surveying British and Chinese rule with equal
scrutiny.

FILMS

Lessons in Dissent, **directed by Matthew Torne, released in 2014**
Before Joshua Wong was the globally recognized symbol of the Umbrella
Movement, he was a fifteen-year-old who led the charge against the
propagandistic curriculum reform effort in Hong Kong's schools known
as moral and national education. *Lessons in Dissent* follows Wong and his
colleagues during this 2012 action, giving worthwhile background for
understanding the motivations of a new generation of Hong Kong activists.

Raise the Umbrellas, **directed by Evans Chan, released in 2016**
Chan's documentary made waves when the Asia Society forbade its
screening in Hong Kong in 2016 on the grounds of political concerns.
The film is an authoritative, gripping portrait of the Umbrella Movement,
unsparing in its depiction of the political conflict and the controversies
that propelled it. It includes memorable interviews with as well as samples
of music by the singers Denise Ho and Anthony Wong Yiu-ming.

CHAPTER FOUR

Richard C. Bush, *Hong Kong in the Shadow of China—Living with the Leviathan*. Washington: Brookings Institution, 2016
Bush's book places the political unrest in Hong Kong in the 2010s in the larger context of an increasingly unlivable life in the city. Bush, who directs the Brookings Institution's Center on East Asia Policy Studies, pays close attention to Hong Kong's economic situation under Chinese rule, both at the highest level and in its consequences for everyday Hong Kongers.

Elizabeth Economy, *The Third Revolution: Xi Jinping and the New Chinese State*. New York: Oxford University Press, 2018
To understand Hong Kong's political situation, you must understand the contemporary Chinese state, and to understand the contemporary Chinese state, you must understand Xi Jinping, who has led the country since November 2012. Economy takes us into how Xi has centralized his power while also providing a good introduction to the Communist Party's increasing global clout and increasing moves to limit freedoms domestically.

Kong Tsung-gan, *As Long as There is Resistance, There is Hope: Essays on the Hong Kong Freedom Struggle in the Post-Umbrella Era, 2014–2018*. Hong Kong: Pema Press, 2019
A sort of postscript to his memoir on the Umbrella Movement, here Kong reflects on the agitations and unrest that continued to tremble in Hong Kong after the events of 2014.

Christine Loh and Richard Cullen, *No Third Person: Rewriting the Hong Kong Story*. Hong Kong: Abbreviated Press, 2018
Loh, a well-known Hong Kong politician, and Cullen, a law professor at the University of Hong Kong, engage questions of Hong Kong identity under Chinese rule in this short book. The future of this identity, they argue, will be decided in the confrontation—in whatever form it takes—between Hong Kong and mainland China. A work that argues for an approach very different from that espoused by activists in 2014 and even more so in 2019.

Ma Jian, *China Dream*, translated by Flora Drew. London: Chattus & Windus, 2018
Ma's biting satirical novel illustrates the mundane dystopia of life in contemporary China. Ma, who lives in Britain and is banned from entering his home country, weaves a story that is in equal parts hilarious and saddening, following a government bureaucrat who heads the state office

102   responsible for replacing civilians' nighttime dreams with propagandistic
       tributes to Xi Jinping.

Chris Patten, *First Confession: A Sort of Memoir*. New York: Penguin, 2017

In his second autobiographical effort, Patten takes us across his long career
as a public official. His appointment as Hong Kong's last governor is just
another twist in this saga, and here he recounts more of the story he began
in *East and West*.

Joshua Wong, *Unfree Speech: The Threat to Global Democracy and Why We Must Act Now,* translated by Jason Y. Ng. London: WH Allen, forthcoming February 2020

The young activist's first book, which appeared in Chinese well before
the 2019 protest wave began, takes the form of a manifesto. In it, Wong
demands that the international audience turn its attention to Hong Kong,
where the decline of civil liberties could be a harbinger of a darker world
to come.

FILMS

China's Artful Dissident, directed by Danny Ben-Moshe, 2019

A deeply engrossing look at Badiucao, a street artist and cartoonist exiled
from his native China for his unflinching critiques of the government.
Since the film was completed, he has been active in international efforts
to raise awareness about protest and repression in Hong Kong and created
many works of art relating to events there.

Joshua: Teenager vs. Superpower, directed by Joe Piscatella, 2017

A Netflix documentary that follows the Umbrella Movement through
the eyes of its most prominent figure. Includes enlightening interviews
with Jason Y. Ng and Clay Shirkey who offer useful insight into Hong
Kong's contemporary dilemmas, as well as extensive footage featuring the
eponymous activist and his colleagues and friends. (Note: The author is
among the analysts interviewed on film.)

Last Exit to Kai Tak, directed by Matthew Torne, 2018

Torne, who first chronicled Hong Kong in 2014's *Lessons In Dissent,* updates
the narrative by documenting the experiences and perspectives of several
Hong Kong political figures, including Joshua Wong. An abundance of
footage collected over Torne's years of work in Hong Kong make for a
gripping film.

China Heritage, "The Best China" (on Hong Kong), http://chinaheritage
.net/the-best-china/
A collection of perspectives on Hong Kong life against the uncertainty of
its future, capturing various attempts at preserving individualism against
China's increasing encroachment. The editor of *China Heritage,* Geremie R.
Barmé, who introduces and translates many contributions to this series,
is one of the world's leading scholars of Chinese culture and history and
someone who has been engaged with Hong Kong issues since the late 1970s.

Helen Siu's contributions to 2017 and 2019 *ChinaFile* **conversations,**
http://www.chinafile.com/contributors/helen-siu
While many commentaries on Hong Kong that have appeared on *ChinaFile,*
a site run out of the New York office of the Asia Society, are good, Siu's
perspective is especially valuable. An anthropologist with posts at both
Yale and the University of Hong Kong, she brings to her writings here and
elsewhere the skills of a top ethnographer and someone with a lifelong
engagement with life and culture in all parts of the Pearl River Delta.

WORK BY JOURNALISTS ON THE GROUND

The following reporters and freelance writers, listed in alphabetical order,
are among those whose published writings, radio reports, and/or tweets
I have found particularly valuable while working on this book (with bold
face demarcating the people I have drawn on most heavily): Wilfred Chan,
Yuen Chan, **Karen Cheung, Antony Dapiran,** Jiayang Fan, Emily Feng,
James Griffiths, Benjamin Haas, Brian Hioe, Rosemarie Ho, **Mary Hui,**
Natasha Khan, Anthony Kuhn, Lily Kuo, Jeffie Lam, **Louisa Lim,** Shibani
Mahtani, **Timothy McLaughlin,** Aaron McNichols, Amy Qin, **Austin**
Ramzy, Ilaria Maria Sala, Suzanne Sataline, Isabella Steger, Alice Su,
Sue-Lin Wong, **Elaine Yu,** and Verna Yu. In addition, the *TIME* Asia team
was particularly helpful to me in understanding events of 2014–2018
and has been valuable again in 2019, and the editors of and contributors
to the *Hong Kong Free Press* deserve a special mention, as they have been
providing an absolutely essential resource for those following events in
the city and continue to do so.

SHORT VIDEOS

Denise Ho speaking at the U.N., uploaded by *South China Morning Post,* July
9, 2019, https://www.youtube.com/watch?v=k6qny5ScUSg

"What Hong Kong Protests Look Like Inside of China," produced by *Quartz*, June 19, 2019, https://www.youtube.com/watch?v=EpFE4900__8

"Video: The Wonderful World of Sham Shui Po," *Hong Kong Free Press*, August 7, 2019, https://www.hongkongfp.com/2019/08/07/video-wonderful-world-sham-shui-po/

NOTES

CHAPTER ONE

13   Checkpoint Charlie is now a museum: Fittingly, the places mentioned are located near enough to each other that a tourist interested in the Cold War can finish off a day of sightseeing in Berlin that begins with a visit to Checkpoint Charlie and includes a climb up the old guard tower with a stop at a museum devoted to the history of espionage, which opened in 2015 and includes exhibits on everything from old and new surveillance techniques to popular culture portrayals of spies in works ranging from James Bond films to le Carré novels. (My thanks to Didi Kirsten Tatlow for telling me about the Spy Museum and suggesting I visit it in May 2019.)

14   except that their internet connection will likely be faster than they are used to: I was reminded of the unusually high quality of internet service in Hong Kong while researching this book, when I visited London and then Hong Kong within the same two-week period in the spring of 2019. While taking the Tube to Heathrow at a time when I did not have a smartphone with a local data plan, I asked a man next to me who looked as though he was surfing the web if he minded checking online to see which terminal my flight was leaving from. He said, without knowing anything about my interests: "I can't get any service on the train; we aren't in Hong Kong!" After I explained that I was working on a book about

Hong Kong, he told me that he was a British expatriate working in the insurance field there and about to fly back there. It was true that throughout my stay in Hong Kong soon after that, I was able to surf the internet on all the MTR trains I took.

15   the longest sea crossing in the world: A note in the British National Archive shows that the idea of creating a driving route between Hong Kong, Macau, and nearby mainland cities was proposed at least as far back as 1986. See Research Department Note No. 20: China's Special Economic Zones and Open Coastal Cities, Far Eastern Section, Research Dept, FCO, Sep. 1986: "Plans exist for a motorway to connect Hong Kong, Shenzhen, Canton, Macau, and Zhuhai."

15   Jonathan Choi Koon-shum, chairman of the local Chinese General Chamber of Commerce: Quoted in Paul Yeung, "Risk-taking Pioneers Will Strike Gold in Bay Area," *China Daily*, UK edition, May 24, 2018.

16   new transportation routes were making it less obvious when one moves from one part of the Pearl River Delta to another: Lily Kuo, "'This Is Part of the Plan': New Train Blurs Line Between China and Hong Kong," *Guardian,* October 4, 2018.

17   For them, the mainland having direct and total control over part of a train station located in the heart of Hong Kong conjures a sense of outrage: It is noteworthy that, while Hong Kong used to be a favorite place for dissidents leaving the Chinese

106 mainland, now they are more likely to pick Berlin as a destination.

17   Some of the men were pressured into making televised "confessions": On indications that the confessions were coerced, see, for example, Emily Rauhala, "Hong Kong Bookseller's Televised Confession Was Absurd and Incoherent—And That's the Point," *Washington Post*, January 18, 2016. For an overall account of the disappearing booksellers and the impact of the case, see Michael Forsythe, "If China Meant to Chill Hong Kong Speech, Booksellers' Case Did the Job," *New York Times*, November 4, 2016.

18   The protest leader Agnes Chow: A note on names: Many Hong Kongers identify themselves by using a Western personal name (that goes first), a family name (placed in the middle), and a Cantonese personal name (that comes last). For clarity and consistency's sake, I have used the Western naming format—the individual's Western personal name first, followed by their surname—except when the individual does not use a Western first name (for example, Chan Kin-man).

18   to borrow the title of a valuable 2017 book: Antony Dapiran, *City of Protest: A Recent History of Dissent in Hong Kong*, Penguin Random House Australia, 2017.

19   References to disappearances figured in many of the interviews: It is worth noting that the theme of "disappearance" is a central and eponymous one in the most influential work of cultural theory dealing with Hong Kong that was published in 1997, Ackbar Abbas's *Hong Kong: Culture and the Politics of Disappearance* (Hong Kong: Hong Kong University Press, 1997). Several people I interviewed for this book brought it up when I mentioned my interest in the topic of disappearances.

19   We asked people to name a novel or film that captured something important about Hong Kong's situation: Ma Jian also mentioned Ismail Kadare's *The Palace of Dreams*, a dystopian novel set ostensibly in the Ottoman Empire but which is also a comment on the modern totalitarian state— in particular, the Soviet bloc. The novel's setting is a state in which the government has access to the citizens' dreams and can mete out punishments for dreams containing insubordinate symbols or metaphors.

20   tracing their roots back to distant places ranging from India to, in the case of her own family, continental Europe: Some families who came to Hong Kong from South Asia have deep ties and a strong sense of attachment to the city; for an eloquent essay illustrating this point by the former editor of *TIME*'s Asian edition, written during the height of the Umbrella Movement, see Zoher Abdoolcarim, "Fighting for the Hong Kong Dream," published online via Time. com on October 23, 2014, available online at http://1in99percent. blogspot.com/2014/10/

time-fighting-for-hong-kong-dream.html.

21   repression in Xinjiang as well as Tibet: The idea of comparing Tibet and Hong Kong is not completely new. See, for example, Isabel Hilton, *The Search for the Panchen Lama* (New York: Norton, 2001), in which, on p. 120, the author aptly describes the "Seventeen Point Agreement" that was forced on Tibetan leaders in 1950 and which led to the creation of a "Tibet Autonomous Region" within the People's Republic of China as one that claimed to offer to Tibet "a system very similar to that" offered "to Hong Kong forty years later— known in the case of Hong Kong as 'One Country, Two Systems.'" See also the following archival source: British National Archive at Kew Gardens: Unclassified memo, responses to HKD contributions for the adjournment debate on human rights in China, Oct. 1992: "What the Chinese are doing in Tibet they will do in Hong Kong after 1997." The Joint Declaration, an international treaty registered at the UN, lays down a series of guarantees for human rights in Hong Kong after 1997. For example, it provides that "Rights and freedoms, including those of the person, of speech, of the press, of assembly, of association . . . of religious belief . . . will be protected by law." For an important early use of the analogy by a local writer, see the following lines from a 1988 text by Ni Kuang: "I've Seen the Future," which Geremie R. Barmé and Linda Jaivin translated and included in their edited volume *New Ghosts, Old*

Dreams: Chinese Rebel Voices (New York: Crown, 1992), pp.431–432: "We must harbor no illusions about this business of there being 'no change for fifty years' . . . What's happening to Hong Kong is exactly like what happened to Tibet when it signed the 'Agreement on Measures for the Peaceful Liberation of Tibet' [under duress on 23 May 1951]."

22   the thirtieth anniversary of 1989's June Fourth Massacre: I prefer the term June Fourth Massacre or simply "June Fourth," which matches up with the Chinese one (following a long-standing tradition in China of calling major historical events after the dates on which they occur), over "Tiananmen Square Massacre," which is often used in the West. One problem with the most common English language name for the event is that the main killing fields were the streets near to Tiananmen Square, not that plaza itself, and Chinese Communist Party propagandists are fond of using the paucity of evidence of deaths at that specific locale to cast doubts on whether there was a massacre at all. There was.

22–23   authorities have even moved to curtail private mourning of the martyrs in cities such as Beijing: There is one part of the People's Republic other than Hong Kong where a vigil is held: Macau, the former Portuguese colony that became a Special Administrative Region in 1999. But even though there was a large gathering in Macau immediately after the June Fourth Massacre to express outrage at the killings in Beijing, attendance at Macau gatherings linked to Tiananmen have tended to number only in the hundreds since 1999, while tens of thousands often go to Victoria Park.

23 **surpassed the size of the crowd in the last couple of years:** There was another, much smaller, vigil held in Kowloon on the same evening, organized by some local students. The theme of this vigil was purely to support Hong Kong democracy; speakers voiced what has become a minority theme among younger Hong Kong activists: that Hong Kongers should reject China entirely, including the notion of remembering those killed in 1989, as any sense of a collective identity between mainland Chinese and Hong Kong people should be abolished. There were fewer than a hundred people at this vigil.

24 **characters that are homophones for "send off a dying relative":** I am grateful to Hana Meihan Davis for alerting me to these linguistic issues.

CHAPTER TWO

25 **a "barren island with hardly a House upon it":** I am grateful to Stephen R. Platt for first pointing me to Palmerston's letter; it is discussed in his *Imperial Twilight: The Opium War and the End of China's Last Golden Age* (New York: Knopf, 2018). Various early views of Hong Kong's potential—or lack thereof, as Palmerston was not the only skeptic—are discussed in John M.

Carroll, *A Concise History of Hong Kong* (Lanham, MD: Rowman and Littlefield, 2007).

26 **Queen Victoria complained in a letter:** Frank Welsh, *A History of Hong Kong*, Harper Collins, 1997, p. 108.

27 **The Chinese traveler Li Gui, who visited Hong Kong at the start of an actual trip around the world:** Li Gui, *A Journey to the East: Li Gui's A New Account of a Trip Around the Globe*, translated by Charles A. Desnoyers, University of Michigan Press, 2004.

30 **"China will honor the commitments that she has made with us about the future of Hong Kong because I think she'll wish to be seen to honor them in the forum of the world":** You can listen to this here (roughly twenty-four minutes through twenty-seven minutes in): https://www.c-span.org/video/?12542 -1/bbc-world-service-phone&start =122. The prime minister made her remarks about Hong Kong in answer to a question asking if she had anything to say to the Chinese people. There is also a follow-up question from someone wondering if she would have pushed for different things in the Handover negotiations if she had been carrying them out six years later—in 1990 as opposed to in 1984. The questioner had in mind, for example, the issue of whether she would have tried to get Beijing to agree not to have troops stationed in the territory or tried to get the Communist Party to guarantee a higher degree of democratization. She claims that, overall, she viewed

the British side as having gotten as much in the negotiations as they could reasonably have expected to get.

31 **"... there were the tents and they were put up with Hong Kong money":** "Secrets & Lies," *Four Corners*, Australian Broadcasting Corporation, June 23, 1997.

32 **the anti-capitalist and chaos-prone country it had been decades before:** For an American diplomat's firsthand account of the turmoil of the mid-1960s in Hong Kong, see Syd Goldsmith, *Hong Kong on the Brink: An American Diplomat Relives 1967's Darkest Days*. Hong Kong: Blacksmith Books, 2017.

33 **Many businesspeople expected China's leaders to keep their promises, at least when it came to economic affairs:** For a wrap-up of optimistic comments, see https://www.rferl.org/a/1085232.html—but see also "Fear of What Happens After 1997 Lies Heavily Over the Colony," Jonathan Mirksy, "The Way We Live Now," *Index on Censorship*, January 1997, pp. 140–144.

33 **Then there was the Golden Goose argument:** The Golden Goose metaphor was so widely used that when Doug Bercuter, a Republican representative from Nebraska who was chair of the Subcommittee on Asia and the Pacific of the congressional Committee on International Relations, spoke at a February 13, 1997, session on "Hong Kong's Handover to the People's Republic of China," one of the first

comments he made was as follows: "It is certainly becoming a cliché to say that Hong Kong is the goose that lays the golden egg, and it should be assumed that Beijing has no intention of killing the goose. Nevertheless, I believe that cliché is, for the most part, accurate" (http://commdocs.house.gov/committees/intlrel/hfa43149.000/hfa43149_0.htm). In an interview in the early 1990s, according to a *New York Times* reporter, Chris Patten noted "dryly" when the topic of Hong Kong as a golden goose came up that it is worth remembering that "history is littered with the carcasses of decapitated geese"; Nicholas D. Kristoff, "Fatty Patten's Last Stand," *New York Times Magazine*, February 21, 1993, p. 36.

34 **"The naked truth about Hong Kong's future can be summed up in two words: It's over":** Louis Kraar, "The Death of Hong Kong," *Fortune*, June 26, 1995.

34 **insisted the CCP would "abolish the legislature" as soon as the territory becomes part of China:** Yvonne French, "Hong Kong: Past, Present, Future," https://www.loc.gov/loc/lcib/9707/hongkong.html.

CHAPTER THREE

40 **Danny Gittings, a journalist and legal scholar based at the University of Hong Kong:** Danny Gittings, *Introduction to the Hong Kong Basic Law*, second edition (Hong Kong: HKU Press, 2016), pp. 24–25.

41 **As local scholar Suzanne Pepper often stresses in her work:**

110   Suzanne Pepper, *Keeping Democracy at Bay: Hong Kong and the Challenge of Chinese Political Reform* (Lanham, Maryland: Rowman and Littlefield, 2008); and idem., "Hong Kong's Struggle to Define Its Political Future," In Teresa Wright, ed., *Handbook of Protest and Resistance in China* (Cheltenham: Edward Elger, 2019), pp. 378–393; and idem., "Hong Kong Protesters are Winning Without Even Knowing It. But What Next for the Movement?" *Hong Kong Free Press*, July 28, 2019.

42   **when the July demonstration took place:** "Huge Protest fills HK Streets," CNN, July 2, 2003.

42   **The economy of Hong Kong:** Most of the economic figures on Hong Kong come from Simon Cartledge's *A System Apart: Hong Kong's Political Economy from 1997 Until Now*, Penguin Random House Australia, 2018, pp. 11–24.

43   **Youth unemployment:** https://tradingeconomics.com /hong-kong/youth-unemployment -rate.

44   **There were calls as well to make the Legislative Council more truly democratic by 2020:** The "promise" was actually postponed at other points before the most recent case. According to the Basic Law, Hong Kongers were allowed to change the procedures at any point from 2007 on. But in 2004, Beijing refused to give a green light to implementing universal suffrage to elect the chief executive in 2007. The promoters of democracy began pushing again for major electoral changes in 2012. The call was rejected again by Beijing.

49   **who sometimes found inspiration in the same places:** For the role of Christianity in general in inspiring protesters of different generations, with references to both Reverend Chu and Joshua Wong's cases as illustrations, see the text and audio of Morgan Lee, "The Christian Backstory of Hong Kong's Pro-Democracy Protests," *Christianity Today*, May 30, 2019.

50   **WTO protesters had been using militant tactics and ratcheting up tensions before the tear gas was used:** Tom Burgis and Jonathan Watts, "Global Trade Riots Rock Hong Kong," *Guardian*, December 17, 2005. For a brief summary of the riots of 1966–1967, see Dapiran, *City of Protest*, and for an illuminating firsthand account by the leading U.S. diplomatic officer on the scene at the time, see Syd Goldsmith, *Hong Kong on the Brink: An American Diplomat Relives 1967's Darkest Days* (Hong Kong: Blacksmith Books, 2017).

51   **The symbolism of umbrellas also has added meaning in Hong Kong:** Gwynn Guilford, "Here's Why the Name of Hong Kong's 'Umbrella Movement' Is So Subversive," *Quartz*, October 22, 2014; I am grateful to Chit Wai John Mok for reminding me of the connection between the street name and a term for umbrella, which is referred to as well in Sebastian Veg's seminal essay, "Creating a Textual Public Space: Slogans and

Texts from Hong Kong's Umbrella Movement," *Journal of Asian Studies* 75:3 (August 2016), pp. 673–703.

52   Several years after the Occupy Movement, Tai wrote: Benny Tai, "30 Years After Tiananmen: Hong Kong Remembers," *The Diplomat*, May 1, 2019.

56   There had even been a dialogue between protest leaders: Liam Fitzpatrick, "TV Face-Off Dramatizes Gulf Between Hong Kong Protesters and Officials," *TIME*, October 21, 2014.

CHAPTER FOUR

58   In February 2016, a conflict broke out in Mong Kok: On the "Fishball" incidents, see Jason Y. Ng. "Never Underestimate the Little Guy: What the Mong Kok Clashes Have in Common with Arab Spring," *Hong Kong Free Press*, February 10, 2016; and Dapiran, *City of Protest*.

63   Law stressed that what he sought for Hong Kong was not to have it become its own country but to gain "high autonomy, a fair political system, and social justice": Nash Jenkins, "The Rule of Nathan Law: Talking Freedom, Democracy and Neckties With Hong Kong's Youngest Ever Legislator," *TIME* September 7, 2016.

68   protesters pasted one of his famous quotes on posters around the city: "A revolution is not a dinner party": See, for instance, https://twitter.com/Nectar_Gan /status/1160037425839628288.

70   "liberty without democracy," as Chris Patten had put it: Dapiran, *City of Protest*.

CHAPTER FIVE

74   "If Carrie Lam isn't concerned about 130,000 people": Holmes Chan, "'No Evil Law': Democrats Hope to Rally 300,000 Hong Kongers to Fresh Protest against Extradition Law on June 9," *Hong Kong Free Press*, May 21, 2019.

74   many think was the largest protest in Hong Kong's history: Organizers claimed that almost two million people marched (compared with closer to one million the week before), while the police estimate was that 338,000 attended that event (compared to 240,000 the preceding Sunday). For comments on the difficulty of getting an accurate count, which also brings in an independent estimate that falls between the two extreme numbers but is not presented as by any means the final word, see "Measuring the Masses: The Contentious Issues of Crowd Counting in Hong Kong," Reuters, June 20, 2019. One point made in this article, which is accompanied by many illustrations and filled with good points about what makes estimating crowd size particularly hard in Hong Kong, is that while organizer and police estimates always diverge, they have been doing so more dramatically of late and that is noteworthy. "I think," one expert they quote says, "the gap between the organizers and police becoming wider is a reflection of how much distrust is in the community.

112   The wider the gap, the wider
        distrust."

76   **protest actions "took place
in seven districts" spread across
the territory:** Helen Regan, Joshua
Berlinger, Jessie Yeung, and Ben
Westcott, "City-wide Strikes Bring
Hong Kong to a Standstill," CNN,
August 6, 2019.

79   **"The Frogs of Hong Kong have
all been in one big pot and the water
temperature has gradually been
rising":** Translated by Geremie R.
Barmé in his "Like Water, Boiling
Water," *China Heritage*, August 15,
2019.

80   **As the poet, translator,
and editor Tammy Ho:** On the
Cantonese version of this song, see
Tammy Ho Lai-Ming, "Who Hasn't
Spoken Out?", *Asian American
Literary Review* 5:2 (Fall/Winter
2014), 173–175. That essay also has
a poignant commentary on the toll
divides over Hong Kong issues were
taking in 2014 within her own family.
Throughout the 2019 movement, Ho
has been writing and then posting
online verses and prose poems that
detail events taking place in her city;
for samples, see Andrea Lingenfelter,
"At This Moment, Everyone is a
Revolution: The Poems of Tammy
Ho Lai-Ming and the Hong Kong
Crisis," *BLARB* (blog of the Los
Angeles Review of Books), August
4, 2019; available online at https://
blog.lareviewofbooks.org/poetry
/moment-everyone-revolution
-poems-tammy-ho-lai-ming-hong
-kong-crisis/.

EPILOGUE

85   **urged one another to "be
water," to adapt their tactics
continually to changing
circumstances:** For an image of
a 2014 poster referring to what it
means to "be water," see Sebastian
Veg, "Creating a Textual Public
Space: Slogans and Texts from the
Umbrella Movement," *Journal of
Asian Studies*, reprinted in N. Ma
and E. W. Cheng (eds.), *The Umbrella
Movement: Civil Resistance and
Contentious Space in Hong Kong*,
Amsterdam University Press, 2019,
pp. 149–181, photo on p. 174.

86   **There's also the metaphor
of the hundred-year flood:** Adam
Hochschild, "America's Real War:
A Political 100-Year Flood," *Salon*,
August 3, 2019.

Columbia Global Reports is a publishing imprint from Columbia University that commissions authors to do original on-site reporting around the globe on a wide range of issues. The resulting novella-length books offer new ways to look at and understand the world that can be read in a few hours. Most readers are curious and busy. Our books are for them.

Subscribe to Columbia Global Reports and get six books a year in the mail in advance of publication. globalreports.columbia.edu/subscribe